The Complete

Venison Cookbook

From Field to Table

Jim & Ann Casada

Published by

High Country Press

1250 Yorkdale Dr.
Rock Hill, SC 29730-7638
www.jimcasadaoutdoors.com

Requests for permission to make copies of any part
of this book should be made to High Country Press at www.
jimcasadaoutdoors.com.

International Standard Book Number
978-0-9856721-1-9

Dedication

For our parents, the late Earnest and Lucy Fox,

and the late Commodore and Anna Lou Casada.

Table of Contents

Acknowledgements

As is ever the case with an undertaking of this length and scope, we owe debts of gratitude to many family members and friends. The book is dedicated to our parents. Ours was the good fortune to grow up in rural homes where closeness to the good earth and enjoyment of its bounty were integral parts of everyday life.

Our daughter, Natasha, has tolerated far more talk of deer hunting and venison recipes than she might have wished, but with each passing year she shows encouraging signs of being more closely attuned to the wild world. We both appreciate her patience and understanding while this book was in progress, and she even offered her father some needed prompting as the project moved towards its conclusion.

We certainly owe thanks to Deborah Faupel and the other folks at Krause who were a part of this work's production. Similarly, we are indebted to those who shared suggestions, recipes, and related information along the way. They included Gene and Roy Turner, Gail Wright, Eddie Salter, Lee Maynard, Tanya Long, Anita Pennell, Deborah Love, Etah Kirkpatrick, Kelly and Janice Reiser, Brenda Palmer, Kathy and Roy Wilson, Gary Cook, Jack Kotrous, and Teresa Rector.

Finally, we would be remiss if we failed to acknowledge all those friends and acquaintances in the deer-hunting fraternity, not to mention ethical deer hunters everywhere, who realize that proper utilization of one's kill is an vital part of the sportsman's role.

Introduction

Of Man and Deer

From earliest times, long before man began to leave written records, deer have been an important part of our diet. Cave paintings in locations scattered across the globe depict prehistoric man and the way he gloried in the quest. We are and always have been predators, and to suggest otherwise is to ignore the accumulated weight of evidence the past affords. Still, the evolution of how man has hunted and utilized deer is interesting in that the story is one of considerable change.

Prehistoric man hunted, and hunted hard, though his success in taking deer was anything but predictable. He hunted not for sport but for sustenance and survival, and to him any method which worked was "fair chase." Or, to put matters another way, thoughts of ethical hunting never entered his mind. That being duly recognized, our distant forebears were in some senses the most ethical of all hunters, for they utilized every animal they killed to the fullest degree possible. All edible portions were eaten. The skins provided clothing and shelter, sinews became bow strings or thread, and bones were transformed into tools. Nothing was wasted, and that is something of which precious few modern hunters can boast.

Until the coming of the Europeans deer and other ungulates (hoofed animals) such as the bison and caribou, were the way of life for many Native Americans. However, by the dawn of the Age of Discovery that situation had long since changed in Europe. Deer, once available to all if they had the skill to kill, had become the exclusive preserve of the rich and powerful, and so to a considerable degree they remain today. That is something we as Americans tend to forget. We take what is really a rare privilege, that of hunting, for granted, overlooking the fact that we are virtually unique in that regard in the modern world (Canada is the only country where really comparable opportunities exist for the average individual to hunt).

Once Europeans found their way to the New World and launched the westward-looking movement which would eventually see the continent settled from Atlantic to Pacific, the world of the Native American and his way of life were doomed. Yet the role of the whitetail in frontier life should not be overlooked. Many a pioneer family depended, to an appreciable degree, on venison as a food. Harvesting deer meant vital sustenance as well as welcome relief from the drudgery of daily chores.

There was prodigality among pioneers though, and to a degree which the Indians would have deemed unthinkable. Market hunting became a way of life in the late eighteenth and nineteenth century, for there was a constant demand for venison to be served in the finest restaurants of major cities. Also, far too many Americans of that era failed to realize the extent of their ravages on whitetail populations, and in time deer numbers dropped dramatically. This is not the place for a detailed discussion of what ensued, but suffice it to say that venison was not a common item of diet in the first half of this century.

There would have been precious little demand for a cookbook of this sort before 1950. There simply were not enough deer, and on a personal level, both of us remember, in striking detail, the handful of times we actually saw deer in the wilds as we grew up in the 1950s. Today, of course, deer are plentiful to the point of threatening to become a nuisance over much of the country, and the animal's comeback story ranks alongside that of the wild turkey as being the greatest wildlife comeback of the 20th century.

Anyone who has a desire to try the taste of venison likely lives within quite reasonable distance of places where the animal can be hunted with a high likelihood of success. Furthermore, to an extent that is true of no other game animal, hunting has proven to be the vital management tool to control whitetail numbers. Fortunately, venison is as tasty and nutritious as the animal is abundant, and the size of the animal is such that it has the potential to make a major contribution to the table fare enjoyed by any hunter. Likewise, it is heartening to realize that a myriad of potential benefits can come from our killing deer.

There is an ample measure of pleasure, a real sense of accomplishment, in the successful quest, but for the sensitive and sensible hunter the decisive moment is a bittersweet one. It is precisely at that point though, as he contemplates his kill, that he should pause and ponder, suitably full of wonder, what the finality of his act means. Theodore Roosevelt, an avid outdoorsman, expressed it well in his enduring work, The Wilderness Hunter, when he wrote:

> *In hunting, the finding and killing of the game is after all but a part of the whole. The free, self-reliant, adventurous life, with its rugged and stalwart democracy; the wild surroundings, the grand beauty of the scenery, the chance to study the ways and habits of the woodland creatures—all these unite to give to the career of the wilderness hunter its peculiar charm. The chase is among the best of all national pastimes; it cultivates that vigorous manliness for the lack of which in a nation, as in an individual, the possession of no other qualities can possibly atone.*

One could only wish that Roosevelt had added a few words to stress the importance and enjoyment of eating one's kill, although the historical record should note that he reckoned some of the finest moments of his life to be those spent around the campfire enjoying a fine meal of venison after a tiring but inspiring day afield.

Hunting soothes the troubled soul and fills us with a deep appreciation of the wild world. It also gladdens us with realization that each time we succeed, and this is especially true with deer, we have made a small yet significant contribution to management. After all, without the activities of man as a predator deer would proliferate beyond all reasonable bounds. For those who doubt this, study the history of deer in New Zealand.

It is also heartening to know that with a clean kill we have taken an appreciable quantity of meat which has never known the intrusion of antibiotic-filled needles, dubious dietary infusions of hormones to stimulate unnatural growth, or indeed artificial supplements (dietary or otherwise) of any sort. The hunter can also be pleased in awareness that the food his kill provides is healthy, wholesome, low in cholesterol and fat, and of considerable nutritional value. In short, the taking of any deer is in many senses a cause for celebration, and the recipes which follow are culinary signposts encouraging readers to share in that celebration. That is best done with venison which has been properly handled from the moment of the kill onward, so let us turn to a closer look at the vital matters of how to go about dressing, hanging, and aging your deer.

From Field to Freezer: Dressing, Hanging, and Aging Your Deer

Proper handling of venison is largely a matter of common sense; unfortunately, all too often common sense is a most uncommon commodity. How often, after all, have you heard acquaintances express disdain for deer meat? Normally their comments run something to this effect: "I don't like the wild taste" or "Venison is always dry and tough." Yet with proper care and cooking, venison can be as delectable as choice cuts of beef, not to mention being a lot better for you.

Care begins the moment your deer is dead. The sooner you can remove the entrails and get the body cavity open for cooling purposes, the better. We personally advocate field dressing in the literal sense of the phrase—dress your animal in the field. With a sharp knife designed for the purpose this is a simple task. If you prefer leaving such work to a butcher or someone at your local abattoir, so be it, but you should realize that delay will affect the quality of the meat.

Should you wish to save the liver, heart, kidneys, and other edible parts of the entrails, it is a good idea to carry some heavy duty plastic bags with you in your field pack. Also, to be completely safe (deer can be disease carriers) you should have a pair of long plastic gloves to wear when doing field dressing work. Once you have removed the entrails, making sure to be especially careful to avoid contamination from any fecal matter, stomach contents, or the animal's bladder, place any of the organ meats you wish to save in plastic bags. Use a couple of sticks to keep the body cavity open to allow maximum air circulation.

The next step is to get the gutted deer in a cooler.

Most commercial deer-dressing operations prefer to skin the deer as soon as you deliver it, but if at all possible avoid that situation. The animal will age just as well with its skin left on, and the skin helps retain moisture and prevents the problem of exposed surface area becoming dry.

Aging time varies, and again a potential problem with commercial operations is that they want, understandably, to follow a deer-in, deer-out policy. On the other hand, venison is best if aged at least a week, and our preference is for 10-14 days, especially for larger bucks. The ideal hanging temperature is within a degree or two of 38 degrees Fahrenheit, and that is normally the setting you find in coolers or meat lockers where aging is being done. Anything much higher and you run into a potential spoilage problem, while temperatures closer to freezing do not result in the meat become sufficiently tender.

As a good general rule of thumb, try to get as much in-cooler time as possible, even if you have to pay a bit extra to do so. You will reap your rewards with tastier, more tender cuts of meat.

Speaking of cuts, that will be the next to last decision you have to make in the preparation and processing of your deer.

To a considerable extent, the choice of cuts is a personal matter. Some folks want virtually everything but the choice cuts—backstrap, back hams, and "little" tenderloins—prepared as stew meat or ground up. Others (and we are among them) prefer the wider variety afforded by a mixture of roasts, steaks, cube steaks, ground meat, ribs, stew meat, and the like. Certainly a greater diversity of cuts lends itself to more variety when it comes to table preparation, and this cookbook has been prepared with that in mind.

For the organ meats, if you choose to save them, the aging process is not a factor. You can clean (or have cleaned) and slice the liver, heart, and kidneys with an eye to your plans for their use. For example, if the kidneys are destined for steak-and-kidney pies (a real delicacy but one seldom offered by even the best of game cooks in this country), they should be diced into quite small pieces. The liver could be sliced into individual serving size pieces, or if you wanted to make liver mush it would be ground. Whatever your means of processing, however, it really is not necessary to age the organ meats. Work them up and wrap them on your own without any help from a butcher. Anyway, you likely will find that processors are unaccustomed to dealing with organ meats.

When it comes to the final step of pre-cooking preparation, whether you do it or have it done professionally, good wrapping is a must. If you do it yourself, make sure that immediately prior to wrapping all excess surface moisture or blood is removed with paper towels. This will help avoid freezer burn. Use heavy-duty butcher paper or special freezer paper for wrapping, and individual packages should be of the proper size. For example, a family of four does not want 15 pieces of cubed steak in a single package. For roasts or larger cuts, double wrapping is strongly suggested, and it isn't a bad idea for any of the venison which is to be stored in a freezer.

If you plan to make sausage or have it made, do that immediately after the venison has been ground up. You can buy handy outfits to make and even case your own sausage, or many processors will do this for you. Alternatively, almost anywhere there are large numbers of deer, there are likely to be one or two folks in the area who specialize in the preparation of sausage. This is something you want to monitor closely though, because individual tastes and thoughts on health can vary considerably here. Some palates lean toward lean and mild; others to sausage so spicy as to be wild. Usually some beef or pork fat is added in the sausage-making process, whether the meat being prepared is summer sausage or of the traditional type. Such additions may, to some degree, be necessary, but it also has health implications which we will look at in a bit more detail below.

The sheer size of a deer almost invariably means that you will need to freeze an appreciable portion of the meat, and once the aging, processing, and wrapping have been completed, this should be done immediately. Many commercial processors have the capability of "quick freezing" the venison, and if this can be done it is advisable. Whether or not this is the case, properly prepared venison will keep in your home freezer with normal temperatures from one season to the next without any appreciable deterioration in quality. However, it is wise to clean out any remaining meat each fall as you ready for a new season of hunting. If you have more left than had been anticipated, you can always share with friends, donate the meat to a local soup kitchen or similar agency serving the needy, or maybe have a neighborhood cook-out. Thinking along somewhat similar lines, also make it a point of using all the meat from every deer you take. If your freezer is already fairly full and the temptation to take only the best cuts presents itself, just remember that there are organizations such as "Hunters for the Hungry" which will be delighted to have what you do not want.

Venison and Your Health

A lot is written about the virtues of venison from a health standpoint, and to a considerable degree they are correct. However, it does seem advisable to dispel some misconceptions and sound a few words of warning before turning to the more positive aspects of venison. First and foremost, any woman who is pregnant is probably best advised to avoid eating venison during the course of her pregnancy. This is because of a fairly common, though often misunderstood, disease known as toxoplasmosis. It is most commonly acquired through eating undercooked meat, and freezing meat reduces the likelihood of infection but does not eliminate it. A woman who becomes infected during pregnancy risks major problems with the fetus she is carrying including death, brain damage, hydrocephaly, jaundice, or convulsions at or shortly after birth. To be perfectly safe, pregnant women should not eat venison at all, and they should avoid all contact with the meat. If they do eat it, thorough cooking (until all pinkness is gone at temperature levels of above 165 degrees Fahrenheit) is essential.

This latter point is deserving of particular emphasis, inasmuch as one of the most common problems with venison preparation is overcooking. Many of the recipes below can be ruined or made appreciably less palatable by too much cooking, and that is another reason why pregnant women are best advised to exclude venison from their diet entirely. Additionally, anyone who handles venison should be aware of the basic concerns connected with safe food handling. Your local home extension or agricultural agent should be able to supply you with a useful pamphlet, "A Quick Consumer Guide to Safe Food Handling" (U. S. Department of Agriculture Home and Garden Bulletin No. 248, August, 1995). Also, always observe cleanliness, keep raw meat away from other foods, and avoid the use of wooden cutting boards. When cooking larger pieces of venison, such as rump roasts, you may also want to employ a meat thermometer to make sure you have reached a sufficiently high temperature in the center of the roast. Internal temperatures of 160-165 degrees are adequate for destroying salmonella.

With those cautionary words in mind, mention also needs to be made of the truth about venison when it comes to fat and cholesterol. Often you will hear words to the effect: "Venison is really good for you because it contains no cholesterol." Such statements are simply untrue. Venison does contain cholesterol, and often the level can be higher than that from a comparable cut of beef. There are, however, two major differences. More of the cholesterol in venison is what is sometimes termed "good" cholesterol, and venison contains very little fat. It is a nutritious, healthy, lean meat, and often it is the only "red" meat individuals with heart problems are allowed to eat. A quote from Drs. Jean Mayer and Jeanne Goldberg, who have studied venison's health values in detail, is instructive in this regard: "The meat itself is quite lean. As long as the recipe used to prepare it does not contain large amounts of fat, venison is a good choice for anyone wanting a lean alternative. In fact, because it is so lean, venison has become increasingly popular in the United States."

As for the specifics in terms of calories and grams, four ounces of venison will contain about 185 calories and 7 grams of fat. A comparable sized piece of beef tenderloin would have 320 calories and 15 grams of fat, while beef brisket (which is a cut containing more fat) would have 400 calories and 21 grams of fat. When you look at those comparisons, the leanness and healthiness of venison are obvious.

If you dress and prepare your own game every step of the way, from kill to freezer to kitchen, you can take some additional measures which will help lower the cholesterol level of the venison you eat even further. As an article in The Nutrition Letter for January, 1990, noted, it is necessary "to understand that cholesterol is an integral part of the cell membrane of animals and so the cholesterol content of meat is more closely tied to the membranes of muscle cells than to the fat content of the muscle." In other words, taking time to remove visible membranes will reduce the amount of cholesterol you eat even more.

Those with high levels of cholesterol or related health concerns probably should avoid eating the organ meats from deer. The heart, kidneys, and liver are higher in cholesterol than lean venison, although by the same token we much prefer to eat organ meat from deer as opposed to that from domestic animals.

As for fat, it normally is not too much of a problem because there will not be the dense layer of fat on whitetails one finds on domestic beef or pork. However, deer which are faring particularly well, such as those killed in areas where agricultural crops such as corn or soybeans are a major part of their diet, can carry some visible fat.

Quite simply, it should be removed. It is not healthy, and it also has a strong flavor and will solidify quickly. If you have recipes where some fat is essential (in the making of sausage, for example), use some beef suet or pork fat.

One reason venison is so lean is because the deer leads an active life filled with vigorous exercise in connection with its daily existence. This is precisely why venison, and for that matter most wild game, tends to be tougher and drier than domestic meat. Yet there are numerous ways to avoid toughness and dryness, along with "wildness," the charges normally levelled on venison by those who fail to appreciate how tasty it can be. As we have already suggested, proper aging does a great deal to help in the tenderizing process. This can also be achieved by pounding or beating individual pieces of meat prior to cooking, by cutting through long muscle fibers (this can be achieved by cubing but also through some judicious "scoring" or slicing across the grain), and through use of any of the many means which break down tissues.

The employment of acids to break down tissues, what is normally referred to as marinating, takes many forms. Almost any palatable liquid which contains acid—lemon, lime, or tomato juice; various types of salad dressing; vinegar; wine; and the like—has the potential to serve as a marinade. You will find that many of the recipes below make use of either a homemade or commercial marinade of some type, and you may well want to do some experimentation in this regard on your own. One further way of tenderizing venison, and it also helps avoid overly dry meat, is pressure cooking. However, it is our opinion that pressure cooking has a negative effect on the meat's taste, and we suggest use of a crockpot instead. The slow cooking of a crockpot works especially well on tougher pieces of stew meat while enhancing the flavor, especially if some herbs or spices are included.

How to Use this Cookbook

Ann and I are folks whose lives are closely meshed with the world about us, and for the most part we believe simple ways bring happy days. However, when it comes to cooking, it is our view that there is no reason why the preparation of meals shouldn't provide an ample measure of pleasure in its own right, and on special occasions we enjoy an elaborate meal with a venison dish as the centerpiece. At other times an easily prepared soup or a stew which can be left simmering all day fits the bill quite nicely. Whatever the nature of the meal though, be it a festive one of the "soup to nuts" variety or a quick, nutritious snack on a busy day, we find that there is a special sort of satisfaction to be derived from being truly self-sufficient. Those who hunt and then enjoy the product of their sport know that quiet sense of satisfaction as few others do.

Unquestionably we are being self-sufficient, not to mention walking along footpaths man has trodden since the dawn of time, when we eat venison. It is a meat which demands direct involvement from the field right through to the feast. A meal which is completely a product of your own efforts—an animal you hunted, killed, dressed, processed, and cooked—is something truly special. It is our fervent hope, as you use and enjoy the recipes which follow, that it will be with an appreciation of the noble whitetail firmly in mind. Perhaps, as you savor the sweet taste of success, you will occasionally pause and ponder the nature of your quarry and the meaning of the hunt. To do so, we feel, enriches the mind as surely as venison nurtures the body. In that regard, a few words from one of the wisest of all American outdoors scribes, Archibald Rutledge, are instructive. They come from a story of his entitled "Why I Taught My Boys to Be Hunters." It is a piece all of us who love the quest should read and re-read.

If the sentimentalist were right, hunting would develop in men a cruelty of character. But I have found that it inculcates patience, demands discipline and iron nerve, and develops a serenity of spirit that makes for long life and long love of life. And it is my fixed conviction that if a parent can give his children a passionate and wholesome devotion to the outdoors, the fact that he cannot leave each of them a fortune does not really matter so much. They will always enjoy life in its nobler aspects without money and without price. They will worship the Creator in his mighty works. And because they know and love the natural world, they will always feel at home in the wide, sweet habitations of the Ancient Mother.

Venison roasts were what Rutledge called "standard fare" for Christmas and New Year's feasts at Hampton Plantation, his ancestral home in the South Carolina Low Country, and perhaps this book will encourage those who read and use it to emulate the tradition of associating venison meals with special occasions. However, we would like to stress that venison also has a place, and it can be a prominent one, in simple, easily prepared meals as well. Certainly as authors, cooks, and lovers of venison it is our feeling that venison can be a welcomed part of any meal, be it simple or splendid.

We wrote this work with every intention of it being user friendly, and with that in mind each recipe goes well beyond a straightforward list of ingredients to include detailed instructions on preparation and, in many cases, tips or suggestions which may serve you well in the kitchen or at the camp cook stove. Where appropriate, there are also recommendations of vegetables, wines, or other dishes which nicely complement a given venison entree. There are recipes for every occasion, from backyard barbecues to fine dining of the sort which demands crystal, silver, and fine china. Mostly though, there is good eating. We have personally tried each of these recipes, and they are divided into sections for greater convenience.

We conclude the book with a number of suggestions for a full meal so that you can, if desired, plan an entire menu around some of the dishes offered here. Throughout our foremost interest is in providing recipes which bring you joy both as you prepare and partake of them. An old adage about cookbooks suggests that if a given volume contains a single recipe you really like, it is a good buy. We hope there will be far more than one recipe here which brings you culinary joy.

That being said, all that remains before we get to the matter at hand, the varied culinary virtues of venison, is to wish you happy hunting, good health, and bon appetit.

1

Choice Cuts

The choice cuts from a deer can provide dining "fit for a king," and that phrase is more than a mere literary device. Throughout Europe during the Middle Ages and on into the era of the Renaissance, venison was so prized than only the royalty and nobility were allowed to hunt deer or eat the meat. Even today, in the same part of the world, you will pay premium prices in posh restaurants to enjoy a meal featuring prime cuts of venison. By way of welcome contrast, we, as Americans, hunters, and ordinary folks are privileged to enjoy the finest venison on our household tables. All that is required is hunting success and a small measure of culinary skill.

All the recipes which comprise this opening section focus on what have traditionally been considered the finest portions of a deer—the backstrap, steaks, and roasts. For the most part, the recipes are for main dishes, for that is how prime parts of venison should ordinarily be utilized. However, you will also find some "quick and easy" dishes here, and of course many of the leftovers, especially from roasts, are ideally suited for sandwiches.

Loin Steak with Crab and Shrimp Sauce

**1 lb. loin steaks—cut 1/2 inch
thick
1 tablespoon olive oil
1 tablespoon margarine
Salt and pepper to taste**

Heat olive oil and margarine in large skillet and quickly cook venison loin until medium rare. Place on platter and keep warm. It is best to cook loin after sauce has started thickening.

Crab and Shrimp Sauce

**2 tablespoons olive oil
1/2 pound fresh mushrooms,
sliced
2 cups whipping cream
1/4 cup White Zinfandel wine
1/4 cup margarine, cut into
12 pieces
1/2 pound surimi crabmeat
(or real crab)
12 medium shrimp, cooked
and shelled**

Heat two tablespoons oil in large skillet. Add mushrooms to skillet and sauté five minutes. Add cream and wine and reduce until thickened (about 10-12 minutes). Season with salt and pepper. Stir in margarine one piece at a time incorporating each piece completely before adding next. Add crabmeat and shrimp and heat through, about one minute. Pour over venison. Serve immediately.

Four servings

Bourguignon Venison

2 medium onions, peeled and
  sliced
2 tablespoons canola oil
2 pounds venison, cut into
  1-inch cubes
1 1/2 tablespoons flour
1/2 teaspoon pepper
1/2 teaspoon marjoram
1/2 teaspoon thyme
1 can (10 1/2 ounces) beef
  consommé
1 can (10 1/2 ounces) beef
  broth, double strength
1 cup burgundy (or other
  hearty red wine)
1 jar sliced mushrooms or 3/4
  pound fresh mushrooms
salt to taste (may not need
  because of salt in broth)

Sauté onions in oil in dutch oven. Remove and set aside. Sauté venison in oil, adding a bit more if necessary. When browned well on all sides, sprinkle flour, marjoram, thyme, and pepper over venison. Then add consommé, broth, and burgundy and stir. Simmer very slowly for about three to three and a half hours and venison is tender. Allow to cook down for intense flavor. Later add more consommé and wine if desired. After cooking, return onions to dutch oven and add mushrooms. Stir well and cook another hour. The sauce should be thick and dark brown.

Serve with a combination of wild and white rice, fresh steamed broccoli, tropical fruit salad, bread sticks and burgundy, of course.

Eight to ten servings

Backstrap in Blueberries

4 venison loin steaks
2 tablespoons margarine
1 cup chicken broth
juice and zest of one large
   fresh lemon (about two table
   spoons)
4 tablespoons margarine
1 cup blueberries (fresh or
   frozen)
several generous dashes
   ground cinnamon
several dashes ground ginger
salt and pepper to taste

Melt two tablespoons margarine in large skillet and cook venison loin steaks to medium-rare doneness. Turn steaks to brown on both sides. Place on platter and keep warm. Deglaze skillet with lemon juice and chicken broth. Cook over high heat to reduce liquid to one-half cup. Lower heat to medium and add four tablespoons margarine. Whisk in margarine one tablespoon at a time. Add blueberries, cinnamon, ginger, salt and pepper. Pour blueberry sauce over steaks and serve immediately.

Four servings

Venison Loin Steak in Brandy Cream Sauce

2 venison loin steaks (8 to 10 ounce each) cut into one-inch thick steaks
2 tablespoons liquid margarine (plus one tablespoon with sauce)
1 cup evaporated milk (I use 5 ounce can light evaporated milk and 3 ounces skim milk)
2 tablespoons brandy
1/2 - 1 teaspoon salt
1/4 cup mushrooms
3 slices small onion, divided into rings

Place two tablespoons margarine in non-stick skillet. Have pan hot before adding venison steaks, onions, and mushrooms. Cook steaks on medium high for 5-6 minutes per side. Inside of steak should be pink. Remove onions and mushrooms when tender. You may need to add about one tablespoon more of liquid margarine while cooking; be sure to have some margarine left in the pan. Add milk, brandy, and salt. Remove venison to serving dish. Cook sauce until thickened and reduced by about half. Stir constantly. Add mushrooms and onions to re-heat. Pour sauce over steaks.

Two servings

Tip: Delicious served with roasted potatoes, fresh broccoli, and fruit salad.

Venison Loin in Tomato Cream Sauce

**1 pound venison loin steak,
 cut into cubes
1/2 cup flour
salt and pepper to taste
2 - 3 tablespoons olive oil**

Dredge venison cubes in seasoned flour. Brown venison in oil; remove and set aside. Prepare tomato cream sauce in same skillet.

Tomato Cream Sauce

**1 medium onion, chopped
1 - 2 cloves garlic, minced
1/2 cup green pepper, diced
 (optional)
1/2 pound mushrooms, sliced
 and sautéed in margarine
1 can tomato soup, undiluted
1/2 cup beef bouillon
1 tablespoon Worcestershire
 sauce
1 cup low-fat cottage cheese
 (or sour cream)**

Sauté onion, garlic, mushrooms, and green pepper. Add soup, bouillon, and Worcestershire sauce. Add venison and heat. Remove from heat and add cottage cheese. Keep warm until ready to serve. Do not boil after adding cottage cheese. Serve with rice.

Eight servings

Tip: By placing cottage cheese in the blender for a few seconds, you can make the sauce creamy without the fat of sour cream.

Steaks with Sherry Sauce

1 pound venison steaks, cut
  into 1-inch cubes
4 tablespoons margarine
1/2 teaspoon salt
dash of pepper
1 clove garlic, minced
1/2 cup chopped onion
1 cup sliced fresh mushrooms

Sauté venison cubes in margarine in a hot skillet. Add onion and mushrooms and continue cooking until vegetables are tender. Add sherry sauce and serve immediately.

Sherry Sauce

1 tablespoon margarine
1 tablespoon flour
1 cup beef broth
1/4 teaspoon garlic salt
1 1/2 teaspoons ketchup
1 1/2 teaspoons Worcestershire sauce
1/4 teaspoon celery salt
1 bay leaf
1/4 teaspoon paprika
pepper to taste
1 tablespoon sherry

For sauce, melt margarine and add flour. Stir until brown. Gradually add broth and remaining ingredients. Simmer for 10 minutes. Remove bay leaf. Pour sauce over venison.

Four servings

Blue Cheese and Mustard Sauce over Venison Loin Steaks

**1 pound venison loin steaks,
cut 1/2-inch thick
1 tablespoon olive oil
1 tablespoon margarine**

Quickly cook steaks in non-stick skillet with margarine and olive oil.

**<u>Blue Cheese
and Mustard Sauce</u>**

**3/4 cup White Zinfandel wine
2 tablespoons finely chopped
green onion
1 cup evaporated milk
1/2 cup beef stock
1/2 cup (1 stick) margarine,
room temperature
4 ounces blue cheese,
crumbled
2 tablespoons Dijon mustard**

Mix wine and green onions in heavy, small saucepan. Boil over high heat until liquid is reduced to two tablespoons. Add evaporated milk and beef stock and boil until reduced to about one cup, stirring often. Blend 1/2 cup margarine, blue cheese, and mustard in food processor. Whisk blue cheese mixture into wine mixture two tablespoons at a time. Simmer until creamy (about three minutes). Season with salt and pepper. Pour over warm steaks.

Four servings

*Tip: Serve over garlic spaghetti. You MUST
like blue cheese to like this!*

Venison Scaloppine with Vidalia Onion and Mushroom Sauce

1 pound venison loin steaks, thinly sliced
3 - 4 tablespoons flour
salt and pepper
1 egg
2 tablespoons water
1 1/2 cups bread crumbs
3 tablespoons olive oil
1 tablespoon margarine

Pound venison between two sheets of waxed paper until thin. Season 3 to 4 tablespoons flour with salt and pepper in pie plate. Beat egg with water in shallow dish. Dredge meat in flour, dip in egg mixture and then roll in bread crumbs. Heat three tablespoons oil with one tablespoon margarine in large skillet over medium-high heat. Add meat in batches and sauté until browned, turning once, about three to five minutes. Transfer to platter and spoon sauce over top or serve on side.

Vidalia Onion and Mushroom Sauce

1 cup chicken broth
1 - 2 tablespoons all-purpose flour
2 tablespoons margarine
1 green vidalia onion, thinly sliced
1 jar (4 1/2 ounce) sliced mushrooms, drained OR 1 1/2 cups thinly sliced fresh mushrooms
1/2 cup evaporated skim milk (or whipping cream)
salt and freshly ground pepper
1/8 teaspoon ground nutmeg
1/8 teaspoon paprika

Combine chicken broth and two tablespoons flour in bowl and mix with wire whisk until flour is dissolved. Set aside. Melt two tablespoons margarine in medium saucepan over medium-high heat. Add onion and sauté until tender. Reduce heat to medium. Add mushrooms and cook three minutes. Stir in broth. Increase heat to medium high and cook until thickened, stirring occasionally (8-10 minutes). Blend in evaporated milk. Season to taste with salt and freshly ground pepper, nutmeg and paprika. Set aside and keep warm. *Four servings*

Southwestern Stuffed Steak

Marinade

3/4 cup lemon juice
3/4 cup vegetable oil
1/4 cup Worcestershire sauce
1 garlic clove, minced
1/4 teaspoon pepper
1 (1 1/2 - 1 3/4 pound) venison steak, butterflied

Stuffing

1 package (8 ounce) frozen chopped spinach, thawed and well-drained
1 jar (12 ounce) roasted red peppers in oil, drained and cut into thin strips
1/2 cup onion, finely chopped
1 can (4 ounce) green chilies, chopped and drained
1 garlic clove, minced
1/2 teaspoon cumin (or more to taste)
1/2 teaspoon chili powder (or more to taste)
1/2 cup shredded Monterey Jack cheese

Place steak in a large ziploc bag. Mix marinade ingredients and pour over steak. Marinate over night in refrigerator. Remove steak from marinade. Spread spinach over steak to within 1/2 inch of edges. Top with red peppers and onion. Combine chilies, garlic, cumin, and chili powder. Spread over pepper and onion layer. Sprinkle with cheese. Roll steak; start at short side. Tie with heavy string at two inch intervals. Place in a shallow roasting pan and bake at 350 degrees for 45 minutes. Let stand five minutes before serving.

Six to eight servings

Tip: Serve with black bean and rice salad.

Venison Schnitzel

4 - 6 venison loin steaks
1/2 teaspoon garlic salt (or
  seasoned salt)
1/4 cup flour
1/4 teaspoon pepper
1 egg
2 teaspoons milk
3/4 cup dry bread crumbs
1/2 teaspoon paprika
2 tablespoons canola oil
3/4 cup chicken broth
1 teaspoon flour
1/2 cup sour cream
1/4 teaspoon dill weed

Pound venison loin to one-fourth inch thickness. Coat with mixture of one-fourth cup flour, garlic salt, and pepper. Dip in egg and milk mixture. Coat with mixture of bread crumbs and paprika. Cook in oil in large skillet four to five minutes per side. Remove to warm platter. Add broth to skillet, stirring to deglaze. Stir in flour, sour cream, and dill weed. Cook until thickened, stirring constantly; do not boil. Serve over steaks.

Four to six servings

Gingered Venison and Peppers

1 pound venison steak, cut
 into thin strips
2 tablespoons soy sauce
2 tablespoons water
1 tablespoon cornstarch
1/4 teaspoon ground ginger
1/8 teaspoon garlic powder

Blend soy sauce, water, corn-starch, ginger and garlic powder and pour over venison. Stir to coat well and let stand for about thirty minutes.

3 tablespoons canola oil
1 small green pepper, cut into
 thin strips
1 small red pepper, cut into
 thin strips
1 medium onion, sliced
3 cups hot cooked rice

In large non-stick skillet over medium-high heat stir-fry peppers and onions in oil for about two minutes. Add venison mixture. Stir-fry until venison is cooked to desired doneness (about four minutes). Serve over hot cooked rice.

Three to four servings

Venison-Cauliflower Stir Fry

2 tablespoons olive oil
1 pound venison steak, cut
  into thin strips
1 small green bell pepper, cut
  into thin strips (optional)
1 small vidalia onion, sliced
1 garlic clove, minced
1 package (10 ounce) frozen
  cauliflower florets (or 2 cups
  fresh cauliflower)
1/4 cup soy sauce
2 tablespoons cornstarch
1 can (14 ounce) beef broth (or
  1 1/2 cups)
1/2 teaspoon sugar
salt and pepper to taste
freshly cooked rice

Slice venison into thin strips. Mix soy sauce and cornstarch well and pour over venison. Stir well and marinate ten minutes while preparing other ingredients. Precook cauliflower in microwave oven for about five minutes or until tender crisp. Heat two tablespoons olive oil in non-stick skillet. Sauté onion, garlic, peppers and steak (adding all soy sauce) until vegetables are tender and steak is brown. Add beef broth, sugar, and cauliflower. Cover and simmer until thickened. Another tablespoon of cornstarch may need to be added. Mix cornstarch with a little water before adding gradually to venison cauliflower stir fry. Add salt and pepper if necessary. Serve immediately over hot rice.

Four servings

Vidalia Venison

4 tablespoons margarine
  (divided)
3 or 4 venison steaks
salt and pepper
1 vidalia onion, sliced
1 cup sliced mushrooms
1 cup red wine
1 tablespoon finely chopped
fresh parsley

Heat two tablespoons margarine in a heavy skillet and fry steaks over high heat quickly (about three minutes per side). Season with salt and pepper to taste. Remove from skillet and keep hot. Add remaining two tablespoons margarine to skillet and sauté onions and mushrooms until tender. Add one cup red wine and bring to a boil to reduce for two to three minutes. Pour sauce over steaks and sprinkle with parsley. Serve immediately.

Three to four servings

Sauerbraten Venison

1 venison roast (about 3
  pounds)
1/2 cup red wine vinegar
1 garlic clove, minced
2 bay leaves, crushed
Pepper to taste
1 envelope dry onion soup mix
ginger snaps, crushed

Place venison in roasting pan. Pour vinegar over roast and sprinkle with garlic, bay leaves, and pepper. Cover and marinate thirty minutes at room temperature turning after fifteen minutes. Sprinkle onion soup over roast and cook in covered roasting pan at 325 degrees for about three hours. Remove roast and strain drippings into a saucepan. Add enough crushed ginger snaps to make a smooth, thick gravy.

Six to eight servings

Steak and Onion Casserole

1 pound venison steaks
  (pound with meat mallet to
  tenderize)
2 - 3 tablespoons flour, seasoned with salt and pepper
1 can cream of mushroom
  soup
1 large onion, sliced
1 can button mushrooms,
  drained
3 - 4 tablespoons canola oil

Coat venison steaks with seasoned flour. Brown in skillet in
hot oil. Remove from drippings
and place in a casserole dish. Top
each venison steak with a slice of
onion. Add soup and one-half
can water to hot drippings to
make gravy. Stir until mixed well
and thickens. Add mushrooms.
Pour over steaks, cover and bake
at 350 degrees for one hour or
until steak is tender. Serve with
hot mashed potatoes or over rice.

Four servings

Venison Casserole

2 pounds venison, cut up for stew
1/2 cup EACH parsnips, carrots, celery, and onion, chopped
1/4 cup canola oil
salt and pepper to taste
1 teaspoon mixed herbs
1 bay leaf
1/8 teaspoon ground nutmeg
1 can vegetable broth (or as much as needed)
2 tablespoons flour
2 tablespoons red wine
4 ounces sour cream
dash of lemon juice

In skillet brown venison on all sides in 1/4 cup canola oil. Place venison in large casserole. Brown vegetables in skillet and add salt, pepper, herbs, bay leaf and nutmeg. Add vegetables and vegetable broth to casserole to cover venison. Cook in 350 degree oven until venison is tender. Do not let venison get dry. Remove meat from casserole and keep hot. Place vegetables in blender and puree. The sauce needs to be thick, so if there is a lot of broth left cook on high heat to reduce broth. Add flour to broth and stir constantly to thicken. Add pureed vegetables to sauce. Stir in wine, sour cream, and lemon juice. Return meat to sauce. Simmer for five to ten minutes to heat through. Taste to adjust salt and seasonings before serving.

Six to eight servings

Venison Antipasto Salad

1 pound leftover marinated rump roast, thinly sliced and cut into narrow strips (or use leftover steak)

1 jar (6 ounce) marinated artichoke hearts

1/3 cup prepared Italian dressing (your favorite)

1 teaspoon dried basil

1 teaspoon lemon juice, fresh squeezed

2 ounces shredded mozzarella cheese

6-8 cherry tomatoes

1 dozen fresh tiny green beans

1/2 yellow squash, thinly sliced

1/2 small zucchini squash, thinly sliced

1/2 cup sliced fresh mushrooms

1/4 cup ripe olives

2 slices red onion, divided into rings (optional)

4 cups torn romaine lettuce

Slice venison and heat in non-stick fry pan if desired (or may be added cold). Wash green beans and microwave three minutes. Add yellow and zucchini squash and microwave two more minutes or until vegetables are tender crisp. Plunge into iced cold water and drain well. Drain artichoke hearts, reserving marinade in measuring cup. Add Italian dressing, lemon juice and basil to marinade, stirring to blend well. In salad bowl combine artichoke hearts, mozzarella cheese, tomatoes, green beans, yellow squash, zucchini, mushrooms, olives, onion (if desired), and lettuce. Add part of dressing and toss. Add venison and as much dressing as you desire and toss again.

Four servings

Tip: Serve with soup of your choice and toasted pita bread for a delicious light lunch.

Greek Venison Salad in Pocket Pitas

1/2 - 3/4 pound leftover marinated rump roast, cut into thin strips and heated slightly in non-stick pan
4 cups torn romaine lettuce
1/2 medium cucumber, thinly sliced
1 tomato, thinly sliced
2 tablespoons crumbled feta cheese
2 tablespoons sliced ripe olives
2 whole pita pocket breads, cut into half

Lemon Dressing
2 1/2 tablespoons fresh lemon juice
1 1/2 tablespoons olive oil
1/2 teaspoon dried oregano leaves
1/4 teaspoon dried basil
1/4 teaspoon garlic salt
1/4 teaspoon salt

Whisk together dressing ingredients and set aside. In medium bowl place torn romaine, cucumber, tomato, crumbled cheese and olives. Add venison strips. Pour dressing over all and mix well. Place a damp paper towel around pita bread and microwave for forty seconds. Cut pita in half and stuff venison salad into pita dividing salad evenly.

Two servings

Tip: May be served as a salad with crisp bread sticks, toasted pita bread or assorted crackers.

Lemon Pepper Venison Steak

4 slices bacon
1/2 large onion, chopped
1 tablespoon sugar
10 (1 inch thick) venison steak
  cutlets from backstrap
juice of 1 lemon
lemon pepper

Fry bacon in cast iron skillet. Remove slices from pan, leaving two tablespoons drippings in skillet and reserve remaining grease. Add onion to drippings and sprinkle with sugar; cook until onion is tender. Remove onion and return reserved grease to skillet. Place cutlets in skillet; squeeze small amount of lemon juice on each cutlet and season with lemon pepper. Cook quickly; meat is best if cutlets are slightly pink in the center. Add crumbled bacon and onion to cutlets and reheat. Serve immediately.

Three to four servings

Tip: Wild rice is a good accompaniment to cutlets.

Venison Steak French Dip

1 pound venison loin steak,
cut into thin strips
1/4 - 1/2 cup Italian dressing
1 can ready-to-serve beef
broth
1/4 teaspoon dried oregano
leaves
2 tablespoons olive oil
1 small green bell pepper, cut
into thin strips (optional)
1 medium red onion, sliced
and divided into rings
1 cup sliced fresh mush-
rooms, optional
4 hoagie (or sub) rolls, split
1/2 cup mozzarella cheese,
shredded
Lettuce and tomatoes, if
desired

Slice steak into thin strips
and cover with Italian dressing (Paul Newman olive oil and
vinegar is good). Marinate steak
about one hour. Heat beef broth
in saucepan and add 1/4 teaspoon
oregano. Place oil in large non-
stick fry pan and sauté vegetables
until tender. Remove vegetables
from fry pan. Drain steak well
and sauté quickly until venison
is slightly browned but still has
pink center (takes only about 1
1/2 - 2 minutes). Add veggies
to re-heat and stir. Split hoagie
rolls and spoon two teaspoons
broth on each side of roll. Top
with mozzarella cheese and broil
until cheese melts. Divide venison steak and vegetables among
rolls. Add lettuce and tomatoes
if desired. Serve with small
bowls of beef broth for dipping.

Four servings

*Tip: It is easier to slice steak thinly
if venison is partially frozen.*

Steaks with Mushroom Sauce

4 venison loin steaks, grilled
   or broiled as desired
1/4 pound fresh mushrooms,
   thinly sliced
1/2 cup vidalia onions, thinly
   sliced
3 tablespoons margarine
1 tablespoon cornstarch
1/2 cup water
1/4 cup red wine
1 tablespoon beef bouillon
   granules
1 teaspoon tomato paste
   several dashes Worcestershire sauce
salt and pepper to taste

Sauté mushrooms and onions in margarine. Dissolve cornstarch in water and add to mushrooms and onions along with remaining ingredients. Simmer until mixture thickens. Serve warm over venison steaks.

Four servings

Burgundy Marinated Steaks

1 1/2 pounds venison steaks

Marinade

1/2 cup oil
1/3 cup burgundy
1/4 cup chopped onion
1 clove garlic, minced
1 teaspoon dry mustard
2 teaspoons red wine vinegar
1 tablespoon brown sugar
1/2 teaspoon basil
1/4 teaspoon marjoram
1/4 teaspoon pepper

Mix marinade and pour over steaks in a glass container or plastic bag. Marinate over night. Grill about five minutes per side.

Four to six servings

Orange Juice Steaks

2 pounds venison steaks

Marinade

6 tablespoons frozen orange juice concentrate
1/4 cup vinegar
1/2 cup oil
2 tablespoons soy sauce
1/2 teaspoon rosemary
1/2 teaspoon celery salt
1/2 teaspoon thyme
1 garlic clove, minced

Mix marinade ingredients and pour over venison steaks. Marinate in refrigerator over night. Cook on grill to desired doneness.

Six to eight servings

Wright Venison Bites

2 to 3 pounds venison steak
2 cups self-rising flour
1 cup white cornmeal mix
1 tablespoon parsley flakes
1 teaspoon garlic powder
1 teaspoon celery salt
1 teaspoon black pepper
1 teaspoon paprika
2 paper grocery bags

Cut the venison into bite-size cubes and soak in ice water for an hour or two. Mix all the dry ingredients listed. Double the paper grocery bags and place mixture in bag. Drain venison in a colander. Remove excess ice. Place the venison in bag and shake. Deep fry for 7 to 10 minutes. Great served with ranch dressing and fresh cut vegetables.

Ten to twelve servings

Gail's Pressure-Cooker Pilau

4 to 5 pounds cubed venison
2 boxes Lipton's onion soup
  mix
2 large jars of button mushrooms
8 cups cooked rice
2 large onions
1 stick margarine or butter
1 teaspoon rosemary
salt and pepper to taste

Mix four cups water and the soup mix in a pressure cooker. Add the cubed venison and cook under pressure for 40 minutes. Chop the onions and sauté until translucent. Add the onions and the remaining ingredients to the cooked venison. Heat thoroughly or place in a large crockpot on low for several hours. More water may be added if necessary.

Twelve servings

Venison Stroganoff

2 pounds venison, cut into
  cubes
1/2 cup celery, sliced
1/2 cup onion, chopped
1/3 cup red wine
1 cup sliced mushrooms
  (fresh or canned)
2 cups beef broth
1 tablespoon lemon juice

Dredge cubed venison in flour to which about 1 teaspoon paprika has been added and brown in heavy skillet in two tablespoons oil. Add beef broth and simmer 45 minutes or until tender. Add other ingredients and cook until vegetables are tender. Serve over rice or noodles.

Six to eight servings

Tip: May cook in pressure cooker to tenderize.

V-8 Stroganoff

2 onions, chopped
2 - 3 tablespoons canola oil
2 pounds venison steak, cut
  into slivers
1 1/2 cups V-8 juice
2 bay leaves
2 teaspoons soy sauce
2 tablespoons Worcestershire
  sauce
dash of Tabasco
salt, pepper and paprika to
  taste
2 cloves garlic, minced
5 tablespoons flour
2 small cans mushrooms
  (save juice)
1/2 pint sour cream
2 cans french fried onion rings

Sauté onions in oil. Pour into deep pot. Sauté slivered venison and pour into pot. Add V-8 juice, seasonings and sauces. Let bubble up and cook slowly about 30 minutes or until venison is tender, but not falling apart. Taste meat for tenderness and don't overcook. Set aside until ready to serve (can be done day before). When ready to serve heat V-8 venison mixture and thicken with flour mixed with juice from canned mushrooms. Add mushrooms and sour cream. Serve on rice or noodles and top with crisp canned fried onion rings.

Six servings

Mustard Venison Sauce

1 pound venison steak, cut into thin strips
2 tablespoons honey dijon mustard
3 tablespoons margarine
1 small onion, thinly sliced
1 (4 1/2 ounce) jar mushrooms
1 (15 ounce) jar spaghetti sauce
1/4 teaspoon oregano
1/4 teaspoon basil
1/4 teaspoon pepper
salt to taste
3 tablespoons sour cream

Melt margarine and mix with mustard using wire whisk. In non-stick skillet brown meat on all sides and mustard sauce. Add onion and cook until tender. Add drained mushrooms. Add spaghetti sauce and seasonings. Cover and simmer about 45 minutes or until tender. Stir in sour cream and heat through. Do not boil. Serve over hot cooked pasta.

Four servings

Venison Parmigiana

1/2 cup flour
1/2 cup shredded Cheddar
  cheese
1 1/2 pounds venison steak,
  cut into 6 serving-size pieces
1 egg, beaten
1/2 cup olive oil
1 onion, chopped
1 (6 ounce) can tomato paste
1 clove garlic, minced
salt and pepper to taste
2 cups water
1 (8 ounce) package mozzarella cheese, sliced

Combine flour and cheddar cheese. Dip steak into egg and coat with flour mixture; brown in hot oil. Place in a shallow baking dish. Sauté onion in oil; stir in tomato paste, garlic, salt, pepper, and water. Simmer 10 minutes. Pour sauce over steak. Bake covered at 350 degrees for one hour. Uncover; top with cheese slices and bake until cheese melts. Serve with garlic bread sticks and tossed salad.

Four to six servings

Paprika Venison

1/2 pound thinly sliced venison loin steak
flour
2 tablespoons margarine
1 tablespoon olive oil
2 green vidalia onions, thinly
sliced
1 tablespoon flour
1/2 cup milk
1/2 cup evaporated milk
1 tablespoon tomato paste
1 teaspoon paprika
salt and pepper to taste

Dredge venison in flour. Heat margarine and oil in non-stick skillet over medium high heat. Add venison and quickly brown on both sides. Remove from pan; set aside. Reduce heat to medium. Add onion and sauté until transparent. Add flour and stir. Stir in milk, tomato paste, paprika, salt and pepper blending well. Simmer sauce until thickened, stirring constantly. Return venison to skillet and heat through. Serve immediately with garlic spaghetti.

Two servings

Venison Stir Fry

1 pound venison steak, cut
   into thin strips
1 tablespoon cornstarch,
   divided
3 tablespoons sherry, divided
3 tablespoons soy sauce,
   divided
1 1/2 tablespoons canola oil
1 onion, sliced
1/2 pound fresh asparagus,
   cut diagonally into 1-inch
   lengths
1/2 pound fresh broccoli, cut
   into small florets
3 tablespoons beef broth
hot cooked rice

Slice venison steak diagonally across grain into thin strips. Place in a shallow dish. Combine two teaspoons cornstarch, two tablespoons sherry, and two tablespoons soy sauce; pour over steak and marinate for ten minutes. Remove steak from marinade. Pour oil into wok or large skillet, coating bottom and sides. Heat to medium high for two minutes. Add steak and stir fry for four minutes or until browned. Remove steak from pan. Add onion, asparagus, broccoli and beef broth. Bring to a boil. Cover, reduce heat and simmer for three to five minutes. Combine remaining one teaspoon cornstarch, one tablespoon sherry, and one tablespoon soy sauce. Add cornstarch mixture and steak to skillet; bring to boil. Cook stirring constantly for one minute. Serve over rice.

Four servings

Pepper Steak

1 pound venison steak or roast, cut into thin strips 1/8-inch thick
1/4 cup soy sauce
1 garlic clove, minced
1 1/2 teaspoon grated fresh ginger
3 tablespoons canola oil
1 cup onion, thinly sliced
1 cup red and green peppers, cut into thin strips
1 tablespoon cornstarch
1 cup water
2 tomatoes, cut into wedges

Combine soy sauce, garlic and ginger. Add venison and marinate two minutes. Heat oil and add venison. Cook over high heat until browned. If venison is not tender, cover and simmer for 30 - 40 minutes over low heat. Return heat to high and add peppers and onion. Cook until vegetables are tender crisp (about ten minutes). Mix cornstarch with water and add to pan. Stir and cook until thickened. Add tomatoes and heat through. Serve over rice.

Four servings

Venison Parmesan

4 venison steaks
1 egg
1/2 cup plain, dry bread
  crumbs
2 cups spaghetti or pasta
  sauce
4 ounces mozzarella cheese,
  sliced
Parmesan cheese

Place each venison steak between two pieces of plastic wrap. Pound gently to flatten each piece to 1/4- inch thickness. Beat egg with one tablespoon water. Place bread crumbs on flat plate. Dip each steak in egg and then in the bread crumbs to coat. Spray a non-stick skillet with vegetable cooking spray and heat to medium-high heat. Cook steaks, turning once, until browned (five to seven minutes). Do not have heat too high because bread crumbs will burn before steaks cook. Spread spaghetti sauce over bottom of baking dish. Place steaks on sauce; top with mozzarella cheese. Sprinkle with Parmesan cheese. Bake until hot and bubbly and the cheese is melted (about ten to fifteen minutes). Serve with pasta.

Four servings

Gary's Loin Strips

1 pound venison loin, cut into strips (about 2 inches by 4 inches)
1/2 cup flour seasoned with salt and pepper
1 egg
1 tablespoon milk
1/4 cup canola oil

Cut venison loin into strips. Dredge in seasoned flour. Beat egg with one tablespoon milk. Dip strips into egg mixture and then into flour again. Heat oil in skillet and quickly brown loin strips being careful not to over-cook. Serve immediately.

Four servings

Tip: These strips can be served as an appetizer with ranch dressing. This is also a delicious method for preparing wild turkey breast strips.

Ranch Venison Parmesan

8 - 10 strips venison loin
1/2 bottle Ranch dressing
1 egg
1 1/2 - 2 cups bread crumbs
1/4 - 1/2 cup Parmesan cheese
2 - 4 tablespoons olive oil

Add one beaten egg to Ranch dressing (liquid dressing; not dry mix) poured into shallow dish. Mix bread crumbs and cheese. Dip venison strips in dressing/egg mixture. Then dredge in crumbs/cheese mixture. Place oil in non-stick fry pan. Have oil hot before adding strips to prevent sticking. Brown venison strips on both sides and serve immediately.

Three to four servings

Venison Pita Pockets

1 pound venison steak, cut
 into thin strips

Marinade

4 tablespoons olive oil
4 tablespoons lemon juice
1 tablespoon prepared
 mustard
1 garlic clove, minced
1 teaspoon oregano

Mix marinade and pour over venison strips. Refrigerate over night. Drain venison and stir fry in non-stick pan over medium high for five to six minutes along with a large sweet onion, sliced. Place in pita pockets with lettuce, tomato, and cucumber dressing. Serve immediately.

Four servings

Fabulous Fajitas

1 pound venison steak, cut into thin strips
1 green pepper, cut into thin strips
1 red pepper, cut into thin strips
1 onion, cut into thin strips
8 flour tortillas, warmed
1 cup shredded cheese (cheddar or jack)
1 cup salsa
1 cup guacamole (or sliced avocado)
1 cup refried beans
1 cup chopped tomato
1 cup shredded lettuce

Marinade

2 tablespoons fresh orange juice
1 tablespoon white vinegar
1 teaspoon sugar
1 large garlic clove, chopped
1/2 teaspoon cumin
1/2 teaspoon oregano
salt and pepper to taste

Combine marinade ingredients and pour over venison strips in ziploc bag. Marinate six to eight hours in refrigerator, turning occasionally. Heat large non-stick skillet over medium heat and stir fry peppers and onions in three tablespoons olive oil about three minutes or until tender crisp. Remove vegetables from skillet and add drained venison. Stir fry for two to four minutes. Return vegetables to skillet and toss to combine. Serve on warmed tortillas with desired condiments.

Four servings

Lime Fajitas

1 1/2 - 2 pounds venison
  steak, cut into strips
1 large onion, sliced
8 flour tortillas (8-inch)

Marinade

1/2 cup FRESH lime juice
1/4 cup olive oil
2 garlic cloves, minced
salt and pepper to taste

Tip: Fajitas are excellent when marinated steaks are grilled to desired doneness and then sliced into thin strips. FRESH lime juice is the secret to delicious fajitas.

Mix marinade in a small bowl and pour over steak. Marinate, covered, in the refrigerator for at least thirty minutes but longer (four hours) is better.

For condiments, choose sour cream, grated cheese, chopped tomatoes, chopped lettuce, pico de gallo, avocados, olives, onion, or salsa.

Prepare desired condiments while the venison marinates. Stack the tortillas and wrap tightly in foil. Heat in a pre-heated 350 degree oven for about fifteen minutes.

Drain venison and sauté in non-stick skillet with sliced onion until done. Place cooked venison and onion in center of warm tortilla and top with de-sired condiments and roll up to eat. Serve with cold mugs of beer.

Six to eight servings

Fondue

Still have an old fondue pot? Find it! Venison is delicious cooked in it. A saucepan will work just fine if you don't have a fondue pot.

1 pound venison loin (or other steak) cut into cubes and placed on a platter. Surround venison with fresh mushrooms for a special treat.

Fill fondue pot with oil (peanut or canola does fine) several inches deep. Heat oil on burner before placing pot on table with alcohol burner or sterno. While oil heats, prepare a few sauces (or use your favorite bottled ones).

When oil is hot, place fondue pot in center of table and spear venison on fondue forks (or skewers) and cook as desired. Serve with various sauces. The mushrooms are delicious cooked with the venison. Enjoy!

Four servings

Mustard Mayonnaise

1 tablespoon mayonnaise
1/2 teaspoon honey dijon mustard (or to taste)

Mix until blended. Serve cold.

Red Sauce

1/2 cup chili sauce
1/4 teaspoon prepared horse-radish (or to taste)
dash Worcestershire sauce
squeeze of fresh lemon juice

Mix until well blended.

Greenbrier Restaurant White Sauce

Equal amounts salad dressing (Miracle Whip) and white
vinegar.
Add black pepper to
taste.

Mix until blended.

Tip: Salad dressing must be used in this. Mayonnaise
does not work as well. This sauce is delicious on fish also.

Horseradish Sauce

1 tablespoon sour cream (fat
free does fine)
1/2 teaspoon prepared horseradish
salt and pepper to taste

Mix until blended.

Low Fat Venison and Seafood Fondue

If you did not like the idea of using oil to cook fondue, here is a delicious alternative for you.

Heat to boiling two cans chicken broth (or beef broth) in saucepan. Meanwhile prepare a platter of your choices of the following cut into bite size pieces: Venison loin steak, shrimp, scallops, salmon, tuna, or any fresh fish fillets, broccoli, cauliflower, potatoes, zucchini, yellow squash, onions, mushrooms. It is important to have everything in small pieces so the cooking time will not be so long. Place boiling broth in fondue pot over alcohol burner or sterno and prepare for a feast as you cook your choices on fondue forks or skewers. Serve with sauces of your choice, such as teriyaki sauce, Dale's steak seasoning, cocktail sauce, or sauce recipes included with other fondue recipe.

Servings depend on amount of items used.

Tip: The leftover broth is great to use for soup.

Marinated Rump Roast

3 pound venison rump roast
3 slices bacon

Marinade

1 bottle Girard's Olde Venice
Italian Dressing (or Romano
Dressing)
2 tablespoons soy sauce
1/4 cup brown sugar

Mix marinade ingredients and pour over rump roast placed in ziploc bag. Marinate six to eight hours in refrigerator. Turn roast several times. Discard marinade. Place roast in roasting pan. Place strips of smoked bacon over roast. Pour 1/2 cup water in pan. Do not cover. Place in 325 degree oven and cook until desired doneness is reached. Slice thinly and pour drippings over slices. Crumble bacon and sprinkle over sliced roast.

Ten to twelve servings

Hungarian Venison Pot Roast

3 - 4 pound venison roast
1 1/2 teaspoons paprika
1 teaspoon salt
1/4 teaspoon pepper
2 tablespoons canola oil
1/2 cup water
1 bay leaf
8-10 small whole white onions
2 (8 ounce each) cans tomato
sauce
8 ounces sliced mushrooms
1 clove garlic, minced
1/2 teaspoon onion salt
2 tablespoons minced parsley
1 cup sour cream (optional)

Sprinkle venison roast with paprika, salt and pepper. Brown in oil in Dutch oven over medium heat. Add water and bay leaf; simmer, covered two hours or until venison is almost tender. Place onions around venison roast. Add sauce, mushrooms, garlic and onion salt. Cover; simmer 50 to 60 minutes longer or until meat and vegetables are tender. Add parsley. Just before serving, remove from heat, remove bay leaf, and gradually stir in sour cream, if desired. Excellent over hot cooked rice.

Six to eight servings

Etah's Burgundy Roast Venison

6 - 7 pound leg of venison

Marinade

2 cups burgundy wine
1 cup beef bouillon
1 medium onion, sliced
1 clove garlic, minced
1 bay leaf
1 teaspoon salt

Place venison leg roast in non-metal container. Cover with marinade and refrigerate for 24 hours. Reserve about one cup of marinade to baste with while roast cooks. If marinade does not completely cover roast, turn roast occasionally to be sure all parts of roast have been in marinade. Remove roast from marinade. Place venison roast uncovered on rack of roasting pan. Place six to eight slices of bacon on roast to cover. Cook in 450 degree oven for 10 minutes. Reduce heat to 325 degrees and cook 15 - 18 minutes per pound basting roast with reserved marinade frequently until roast reaches desired doneness.

Eight to ten servings

*Tip: A meat thermometer is quite
an asset in preparing this roast.*

Clay Cooker Roast

2 - 3 pound venison roast
2 garlic cloves
potatoes
celery
onions
carrots
turnips
thyme
parsley
bay leaf
red wine

Water the clay pot as directed with pot instructions. Peel and slice garlic cloves into thin strips. Cut openings in roast and place garlic slivers evenly in roast. Season roast with salt and pepper. Place in cooker. Place vegetables of choice around roast. Add one-half cup wine, if desired. Top with herbs. Cover and place in a COLD oven. Bake at 450 degrees about 45 - 60 minutes. Time will vary because of oven, shape of roast, and desired degree of doneness.

Eight to ten servings

Tip: If you have a clay cooker, try venison in it. You will be pleased with the moist results. Cooking bags are another alternative to cook venison roasts.

Anita's Venison Sauerkraut Rolls

4 venison steaks
3 slices bacon
1 chopped onion
1 teaspoon salt
1/2 teaspoon pepper
1 cup sauerkraut
1/2 cup beef broth
2 teaspoons sugar

Pound meat until quite thin and cut into pieces about three by four inches. Dice bacon and sauté. Add onions and cook approximately five minutes. Add sugar, salt, pepper, and sauerkraut. Heat thoroughly. Place a portion of sauerkraut mix in center of each piece of meat. Roll and tie securely with thread. Place rolls in a greased 8 x 12 x 2 casserole, add broth, and bake at 350 degrees for about one hour.

Four servings

2

Crockpot Cookery

One of the great joys of cooking in a crockpot is that it places few demands on your time. The ingredients are simply placed in the crockpot and left. Hours later a hearty meal, tasty and tempting after a day of magical mingling of flavors, requires nothing but to be emptied into a serving dish and set upon the table. Voila! All is in readiness.

Crockpot cooking is not only easy in terms of the effort required; it is virtually foolproof. With nothing more than a crockpot, a few vegetables and spices, and a bit of water, even the most inept of hands in the kitchen is suddenly transformed into a culinary genius. The recipes in this section are ideally suited for the busy, working family or for a remote hunt camp where all those in company are anxious to spend their precious leisure hours in a stand rather than over a stove.

Cranberry Roast in Crockpot

1 (3 - 4 pound) venison roast
salt and pepper to taste
1 (10 1/2 ounce) can double
   strength beef broth
1/2 can water
1/4 teaspoon ground cinnamon
2 - 3 teaspoons cream-style
   prepared horseradish
1 (16 ounce) can whole berry
   cranberry sauce

In saucepan heat broth, water, cinnamon, horseradish and cranberry sauce. Stir to break apart and bring to boil. Place venison roast in crockpot. Pour sauce over roast and cook on low six to eight hours or until roast is tender. Pass juice with roast.

Eight servings

Tip: This roast is good sliced cold for sandwiches.

Cranberry Venison Spread

Enough left over Cranberry
   Roast in Crockpot to make 2
   cups venison finely chopped
   in food processor
3 hard boiled eggs
2 stalks celery
10 - 12 pickle chips (bread and
   butter type)
2 tablespoons mayonnaise (or
   as desired)
salt and pepper to taste

Finely chop venison in food processor. Remove. Place eggs, celery, and pickles in food processor and chop finely. Mix with chopped venison and add enough mayonnaise to bind together. Salt and pepper to taste. Delicious served as an appetizer with crackers or on sandwiches.

Anna Lou's Crockpot Roast

2 pound (or larger) venison
   roast
2 tablespoons white vinegar
2 tablespoons orange juice

Pour vinegar and orange juice over roast and marinate over night. Turn roast occasionally. Rinse roast off and place in crockpot. Add 1 garlic clove (minced), 2 beef bouillon cubes, and 1/2 cup water. Cook on low six to eight hours (or three to four hours on high). Check occasionally to see if tender. Remove roast when tender and thicken gravy with 2 tablespoons flour mixed well into one-half cup water.

Triple Batch Roast

4 1/2 - 5 pound venison roast
2 onions, cut into quarters
4 stalks celery, cut into 2-inch
   strips
lots of black pepper
salt to taste
4 - 6 cups water

Place all ingredients in crockpot and cook on low six to eight hours or until tender. Remove roast from crockpot and chop or shred when venison is cool enough to handle. Place in 1 - 1 1/2 pound containers and freeze. Use as needed for various recipes. See: Brunswick Stew, Quick and Easy Pot Pie, BBQ in a Flash, Ten Minute Spaghetti Sauce, Etah's Venison Patties, Creamed Venison, Wild Rice Soup, and Vegetable and Venison Soup.

Crockpot Roast and Vegetables

1 1/2 - 2 pound rump roast
garlic salt to taste
6 - 8 peeled potatoes
6 - 8 carrots, cut into 2-inch
  chunks
1 can cream of celery soup
1 can water with 2 teaspoons
  beef bouillon granules added

Place roast in center of crock-pot. Add garlic salt to taste and other desired seasonings. Place potatoes and carrots around roast. Add one can celery soup and one can water with two teaspoons beef bouillon granules added. Cover and cook on medium six to eight hours or until tender.

Six to eight servings

Crockpot Lemon Venison

1 (2 pound) venison roast, cut
  into 1/2 inch slices
margarine
1 garlic clove, minced
1/2 cup onion
1/2 cup white wine
1 can cream of celery soup,
  undiluted
grated rind of 1 lemon
juice of 1 lemon
1 can (4 ounce) mushrooms
1 (8 ounce) package noodles,
  cooked

In skillet brown venison in margarine and place in crockpot. Sauté onions and minced garlic in skillet. Add wine, soup, rind, and juice to skillet and bring to a boil, stirring until smooth. Add mushrooms. Pour over venison and cook on low four to six hours or until tender. Serve over noodles.

Six servings

Brunswick Stew in Crockpot

1 1/2 pounds boneless chicken breasts (or whatever parts you prefer; we find the leg meat from wild turkey works well in stews and soups)
2 stalks celery, cut up
1 small onion, quartered
3 - 4 cups water
1 pound chopped, cooked venison (from Triple Batch Roast)
1 can (14 ounce) chicken broth plus 2 cups broth from cooking chicken
1 (10 ounce) package frozen baby limas
1 (10 ounce) package frozen whole kernel corn
1/2 cup chopped onion
1 (28 ounce) can whole tomatoes, undrained and chopped
2 medium potatoes, peeled and diced
2 tablespoons margarine
1 teaspoon salt
1/8 cup sugar
1/2 - 1 teaspoon black pepper
1/4 teaspoon red pepper (or to taste)

Combine chicken, celery, quartered onion, and four cups water (or amount needed to cover chicken) in a large stock pot; bring to a boil. Cover, reduce heat and simmer forty-five minutes or until chicken is tender. Remove chicken from broth and chop when cool enough to handle. Remove celery and onion from broth and place two cups of reserved broth in crockpot. Add canned chicken broth, chopped chicken, chopped venison, and remainder of ingredients. Cook on medium six to eight hours or until potatoes and vegetables are tender.

Eight or more servings

Venison Stew in Crockpot

Place in crockpot:

**1 pound venison, cut into
chunks
1 small onion, chopped
2 stalks celery, copped
1 can cream of mushroom
soup
1/2 can water**

Cook on medium-high for three hours. Add the following after three hours (or more):

**4 medium potatoes, peeled
and chopped
1/2 pound carrots, chopped
(or vegetables of choice)**

If venison is tender, lower heat. If not continue to cook on medium-high. About one hour before serving time, add five ounces frozen green peas and salt and pepper to taste. Serve with bread sticks.

Six servings

Crockpot Venison Stew Meat

**1 pound venison stew meat
1 (15 ounce) jar pearl onions,
drained
1 (10 1/2 ounce) can beef consommé
1 (10 1/2 ounce) can cream of
mushroom soup
hot cooked noodles**

Put venison, onions, consommé and soup in crockpot and cook on low six to eight hours. Serve over noodles.

Four to six servings

Deborah's Crockpot Venison Tips

1 pound venison roast, cut
  into chunks
1 can cream of mushroom
  soup, undiluted
1 can beefy mushroom soup,
  undiluted
1/2 package dry onion soup
  mix

Brown venison in fry pan. Add soups and venison to crockpot. Cook six to eight hours on low heat. Serve over hot cooked rice.

Four servings

Shirley's Crockpot Stew

1/2 - 3/4 pound venison roast,
  cut into chunks
1 cup water
1 can French onion soup
1 medium onion, quartered

Cook above in crockpot on high for two hours. Add: 4 medium potatoes, cut into chunks and one cup carrots, chopped.

Cook four more hours on low. Add one package (dry mix) brown gravy mix by placing gravy mix in small bowl and add enough water to mix to dissolve; add to stew and cook until hot. Add more water if needed.

Four to six servings

Venison and Veggie Crockpot

1-2 pound venison roast
1 large can tomatoes
2 cups carrots
1/4 teaspoon garlic powder
1 large onion, quartered
2 ribs celery, sliced
2 potatoes, quartered
1 turnip, quartered
1 teaspoon salt
1/2 teaspoon pepper

Place meat and remaining ingredients in crockpot for six to eight hours on low. Serve over rice.

Six to eight servings

Crockpot BBQ Hash

2-3 pound venison roast
1 cup beef broth
1 bottle barbecue sauce
1/4 cup ketchup
1/4 cup Worcestershire sauce
1 large onion, chopped
1 teaspoon lemon pepper
1/2 teaspoon paprika
Tabasco sauce to taste

Place all ingredients in crockpot on low for eight to ten hours. If you prefer finely chopped barbecue, place roast in food processor to chop. Serve over rice.

Eight to ten servings

Pepper Steak in the Crockpot

2 pounds venison, cut into thin strips
1/4 cup flour
salt and pepper to taste (remember that bouillon granules add salt)
1 large vidalia onion, sliced
2 green peppers, seeded and cut into 1/2-inch strips
1 can (16 ounces) whole tomatoes, undrained
1 tablespoon bouillon granules
2 teaspoons Worcestershire sauce
cooked, fluffy rice

Toss venison strips with flour, salt and pepper to coat thoroughly. Place in crockpot. Add onion, garlic, and half of the green pepper strips. Stir well. Add bouillon granules and Worcestershire sauce to tomatoes. Pour into crockpot and cover venison well. Cook on low for six to eight hours. For last hour of cooking, turn to high setting and stir in remaining green pepper strips.

Four to six servings

Tip: If you prefer a thicker gravy, mix three tablespoons flour and three tablespoons water until smooth and add to crockpot. Cover and cook until thickened.

Crockpot Chili

1/2 pound dried pinto (or kidney) beans
2 (28 ounces each) cans whole tomatoes
1 large green pepper, chopped - optional
1 large onion, chopped
1 clove garlic, minced
2 1/2 to 3 pounds ground venison
3 tablespoons chili powder
3 tablespoons cumin
salt and pepper to taste

Soak beans over night. Simmer until soft. Drain and place in crock pot; add tomatoes, green pepper, onion and garlic. Brown venison; drain if necessary and add to crockpot. Add chili powder and cumin and any other desired seasonings. Mix thoroughly. Cover and cook on low eight to fourteen hours or on high four to five hours. Taste for seasonings and adjust. Serve with grated cheese, chopped onions, and sour cream.

Twelve servings

Crockpot Venison Gravy

1 pound venison roast (or cubed steak) cut into chunks or strips
1 (10 ounce) can mushroom soup
1 (10 ounce) can cream of onion soup
1 soup can water

Brown venison in skillet and place in crockpot. Add soups and water. Stir to mix well. Cook on low four to six hours or until venison is tender and gravy is thickened. Gravy may be thickened with cornstarch if necessary. Serve over rice or pasta.

Four to six servings

Creamed Venison

1/2 - 3/4 cup chopped onion
1/2 cup chopped celery
2 tablespoons olive oil
2 cups chopped venison (use
  leftovers from Cranberry
Roast in Crockpot or Triple
  Batch Roast)
1 can cream of mushroom
  soup
1/2 can water
1 teaspoon beef bouillon granules

Sauté celery and onion in fry pan until tender. Add mushroom soup, one half can water to which bouillon has been added, and chopped venison. Simmer to heat through. Salt and pepper to taste. Serve over rice or toast.

Four servings

Tomato Venison Stew

1 pound venison, cut into
  chunks
1 onion, chopped
2 stalks celery, chopped
4 carrots, chopped
2 - 4 medium potatoes, peeled
  and chopped
1 can tomato soup, undiluted
1 can cream of mushroom
  soup, undiluted

Place above ingredients in crockpot and stir well. Cook on low six to eight hours or until venison is tender. About one hour before serving time, add one package (five ounce) frozen green peas. Serve with hot baked bread.

Four to six servings

BBQ in a Flash

1 container (1 1/2 pound)
  Triple Batch Roast
Maurice's BBQ Sauce - Origi-
  nal Mustard or Quick and
  Easy Barbecue Sauce (see
  recipe)

Place venison in saucepan and add BBQ sauce to taste. Simmer until warm. Serve on warm buns with cole slaw or over rice.

Quick and Easy Barbecue Sauce

1 cup ketchup
2 dashes Worcestershire
  sauce
2 teaspoons sugar
1/4 cup oil
squeeze of fresh lemon juice
4 cloves garlic, minced (or
  less to taste)

Mix above ingredients with wire whisk and use with Triple Batch Roast for BBQ in a Flash instead of a mustard base sauce.

Ten Minute Spaghetti Sauce

1 can (16 ounce) tomatoes,
  undrained
1 jar (14 ounce) prepared spaghetti sauce
1 container (1 pound) Triple
Batch Roast, defrosted
1 teaspoon basil

Place tomatoes in large saucepan and chop up with side of spoon. Add spaghetti sauce, shredded venison, and basil. Simmer until hot while pasta cooks. Serve Parmesan cheese for topping.

This gives a different taste and texture to spaghetti sauce.

Four servings

Etah's Venison Patties

1 venison roast (4 - 6 pounds)
2 onions, quartered
2 celery stalks, chopped
1 bay leaf
salt to taste
water to cover

**For patties you will need
the following:**

6 cups minced venison
3 cups mashed potatoes (boil
   potatoes and mash with 1/2
   stick margarine)
1 cup onion, finely minced
2 eggs, lightly beaten
1/2 teaspoon pepper

Place roast, vegetables, bay leaf, and salt in crockpot. Cover with water and cook for six to eight hours or until roast is tender. Set aside until cooled. Mince venison to make patties. Do not grind or place in food processor.

Mix together minced venison, mashed potatoes, minced onion, eggs, and pepper. Shape into patties. Fry in bacon grease in hot skillet until brown on both sides. (Etah uses an electric skillet at 420 degrees). Serve immediately.

Eight to ten servings

Tip: These patties can be placed on cookie sheets and frozen. Then place in freezer bag and cook when needed. For variety, serve with mushroom sauce over patties.

Quick and Easy Venison Pot Pie

1 1/2 pounds cooked venison roast, chopped (from Triple Batch Roast Recipe)
1 can beef broth
2 cups mixed vegetables (whatever you like)—carrots, potatoes, peas, onions, celery, corn, green beans, limas, etc.)
1 can cream of celery soup, undiluted

Place chopped, cooked roast in 9 by 13 baking pan. Pour one cup (or more if you like) of beef broth over venison. Then add mixed vegetables. I like to precook the vegetables some in the microwave until the largest vegetables are tender. Spread one can cream of celery soup over venison and vegetables.

In another bowl, mix together with a wire whisk one stick margarine (melted), one cup self-rising flour, and one cup milk. Pour over venison and vegetables. Bake at 350 degrees for thirty to forty minutes or until golden brown.

Six servings

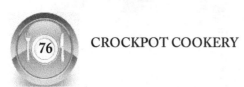

Pennell Bar-B-Que Venison

1 venison roast (3 pounds)

Sauce

1/4 cup vinegar
1/2 cup water
2 tablespoons brown sugar
1 tablespoon mustard
1 teaspoon salt
2 tablespoons pepper
1 large onion (chopped)
1/4 cup butter
**1/2 teaspoon Worcestershire
  sauce**
3 tablespoons liquid smoke
1 tablespoon soy sauce
1/2 teaspoon garlic powder

Simmer in crockpot with one cup water over night or until tender. Mix first eight ingredients in saucepan. Simmer uncovered about ten minutes. Stir frequently. Remove from heat and add remaining ingredients. Pour over venison which has already been shredded. Bake at 300 degrees for at least one and a half hours.

Ten to twelve servings

Pennell Mexican Casserole in the Crockpot

1 1/2 pounds ground venison
1 medium onion, chopped
**1 can cream of mushroom
  soup**
1 can cheddar cheese soup
1 can diced green chilies
1 can taco sauce
1/2 teaspoon parsley flakes
1 pinch oregano
1 pinch nutmeg
**1 package crushed Doritos
  shredded cheddar cheese**

Brown ground venison and onions. Drain, if necessary, and add parsley, oregano, nutmeg, salt and pepper to taste. Simmer for five minutes. Add the rest of the ingredients one can at a time stirring constantly until well mixed. Place in a crockpot at low heat for one hour. Serve over crushed doritos and garnish with cheese.

Six to eight servings

3

Venison on the Grill

Cooking outside on the grill has, over the last two generations, become as American as the traditional apple pie and baseball. It offers an opportunity (or an excuse) for dad to flaunt his flair for cooking, and there is no denying the fact that the aroma and taste of food from the grill will tempt even the most jaded of appetites.

Vension lends itself to grilling in a variety of ways, and many will be surprised at just how versatile the meat is when it comes to the grill. Whether you wish to prepare a meal to be shared on a warm summer's day with some neighborhood friends, top off your opening day hunt with a turn at the grill, or merely take a break from the routine of the kitchen, you will find recipes in this section to fit your fancy.

Backstrap in Bacon

Cut desired amount of venison loin into 1-inch chunks and place in bowl.

Mix equal amounts of water and Dale's Steak Seasoning. Pour over loin and marinate six to eight hours.

Wrap each chunk in bacon and secure with toothpick.

Grill or broil until reaches desired doneness. Do not over cook.

Serve as appetizer.

Tip: Our daughter who is not particularly fond of venison came home with this recipe after visiting a friend. She was surprised to find that she really liked venison prepared in this manner!

Venison London Broil

1 1/2 - 2 pound venison steak

Marinade

1/4 cup oil
1/4 cup lemon juice
2 tablespoons soy sauce
2 teaspoons sugar
1 clove garlic (crushed)

Place steak in a shallow non-metal dish. Mix marinade ingredients with wire whisk and pour over steak. Cover and refrigerate over night (or at least eight hours).

Grill or broil three to four inches from heat for twelve to fourteen minutes. Do not over cook. Cut diagonally across grain to serve.

Four to six servings

Marinade for Grilled Venison Steaks

1/2 cup margarine
juice of two lemons
1 tablespoon Worcestershire
sauce

Melt margarine and add other ingredients. Marinate venison steaks for several hours. Grill until desired doneness is reached.

Blackened Venison Loin Steaks

4 - 6 venison loin steaks, cut
1-inch thick
1/2 - 1 teaspoon cracked black
pepper
1/4 - 1/2 teaspoon salt

Press pepper into both sides of each venison steak. Place steaks on grill (or in broiler pan) two to three inches from heat. Grill (or broil) ten to twelve minutes or until desired doneness is reached. Turn only once. Season with salt when cooking is completed.

Four servings

Pennell's Marinated Loin Steak

1 - 1 1/2 pounds venison loin
steaks
1/2 cup bourbon
1/2 cup soy sauce
2 tablespoons brown sugar
bacon

Mix bourbon, soy sauce, and brown sugar. Marinate venison over night. Wrap steaks with bacon slices securing with a toothpick and grill until cooked to desired doneness. Do not over cook.

Four servings

Venison Steaks with Jezebel Sauce

Jezebel Sauce

Equal amounts of:
 apple jelly
 pineapple preserves
Melt above in double boiler.
Add to taste:
 horseradish
 dry mustard

Grill or broil steaks as desired and serve with warmed jezebel sauce.

Mix well and serve warm on venison steaks. Keeps well in refrigerator. Always reheat in double boiler; never use direct heat.

Tip: The amount of horseradish and mustard depends on how hot and spicy you like your foods.

Venison Steaks with Mustard Rub

1 tablespoon lemon pepper
2 tablespoons dry (powdered)
 mustard
1 teaspoon garlic salt
1 teaspoon paprika

Blend above ingredients in a small bowl. Rub mixture evenly over the surface of venison loin steaks. Grill over medium heat, not hot coals, until desired doneness is reached. Turn only once. Be careful because over cooked steaks will become too dry.

Tip: If you are using a less tender cut of steaks, beat with a meat mallet to tenderize before adding rub.

Venison Mixed Grill

1/2 - 3/4 pound venison loin
  steak
1 cup Italian Salad Dressing,
  divided
1/4 - 1/2 teaspoon garlic salt
1 teaspoon Italian seasoning
1 baking potato, cut into large
  strips
1 turnip, cut into large chunks
1 onion, cut into large chunks
1 zucchini squash, cut into
  strips
6 - 8 small carrots
6 - 8 mushrooms
6 - 8 cherry tomatoes
1 bell pepper, cut into strips
4 teaspoons grated Parmesan
  cheese
salt and pepper to taste

Place venison steaks in bowl and pour one-half cup Italian dressing over and marinate for one hour.

Pierce potato with fork and microwave at high for about five minutes (or until partially done). Cool slightly and cut lengthwise into four wedges.

Microwave turnip for three to four minutes and cut into chunks. Any other vegetables can be pre-cooked in microwave to make vegetables all be tender at the same time.

Cut all vegetables into chunks or strips and place on broiler pan or grill.

Mix one teaspoon Italian seasoning with one-half cup Italian dressing. Brush on all vegetables. Broil or grill four inches from heat for five to six minutes. Drain steaks and sprinkle with garlic salt. Add steaks to grill and turn vegetables. Brush vegetables with dressing again. Cook five to six minutes. Turn steak and vegetables. Sprinkle vegetables with Parmesan cheese and cook for five or six minutes more or until venison and vegetables are done. Be sure not to over cook steak; overcooked venison becomes dry and tough. Season with salt and pepper as desired.

Two servings

Tip: Use vegetables of your choice to vary mixed grill and to make more seasonal.

Teriyaki Steaks

**1 - 1 1/2 pound venison steak,
  3/4 inch thick**
1/2 cup teriyaki sauce
1/2 cup dry red wine

Place steak in a resealable plastic bag,. Pour teriyaki sauce and wine over steak. Seal and refrigerate for three or four hours. Season grill top with vegetable oil. Grill steaks for fifteen to twenty minutes at medium with hood closed. Try to avoid turning steaks frequently. One turn should be enough. Cut steak into serving size pieces and serve immediately. Steak may also be cut across grain into very thin slices.

Beer Marinade for Venison Steaks

1 cup beer
1/4 cup soy sauce
1/4 cup pineapple juice
**1/2 medium onion, finely
  chopped**
1 garlic clove, crushed
**2 tablespoons firmly packed
  brown sugar**
2 tablespoons vinegar
**1/4 teaspoon ground ginger
  (or fresh)**

Place venison in non-metal container and pour marinade over steak. Cover and marinate at least eight hours. Turn venison once. Drain marinade from steak. Grill or broil venison until done being careful not to over cook.

Tip: If using broiler pan, pouring a little water in bottom of pan will make clean up easier because it keeps sugar from burning in pan.

Kathy's Grilled Steaks

1 pound venison steaks
ginger ale or 7-Up

Place steaks in baking dish and pour water over steaks. Remove water periodically until water is no longer pink from blood. Pour ginger ale or 7-Up over steaks and marinate four hours or over night. Cook on grill to desired doneness. Be careful—over cooking venison is the mistake many make.

Marinated Steaks

1 pound venison steaks

Marinade

1/3 cup wine vinegar
2 tablespoons olive oil (or canola)
2 tablespoons soy sauce
1 tablespoon Worcestershire sauce
1 teaspoon dijon-style mustard
1/2 teaspoon garlic salt
1/4 teaspoon pepper

Mix marinade ingredients and pour over venison steaks in ziploc bag. Marinate at least two hours and turn occasionally. Grill over medium hot coals to desired doneness.

Beer and V-8 Marinade

1-1 1/2 pounds venison steaks

Marinade
1 can or bottle beer (7 - 12 ounces)
1 can (6 ounce) V-8 juice
1 onion, chopped
1 tablespoon sugar
1/4 teaspoon celery salt
1/8 teaspoon garlic powder
hot pepper sauce to taste (6 - 8 drops)

Blend marinade ingredients in small mixing bowl. Pour over venison steaks placed in resealable bag. Refrigerate for at least eight hours. Drain steaks from marinade and grill or broil to desired doneness.

Four servings

Gail's Smoked Venison

two-rack smoker
15 - 20 pounds venison roasts, hams and/or loins
20 pounds charcoal
2 cups hickory or mesquite wood chips
2 cups olive oil
garlic salt
black pepper
bacon

Soak wood chips several hours before lighting coals. While the coals are getting ready, coat the venison well with olive oil. Sprinkle venison generously with garlic salt and black pepper. Once the coals are ready, place at least two strips of bacon on top of each roast, ham or loin. Cover smoker and cook ten to twelve hours. Be sure the smoker stays within the ideal temperature range. If the temperature gauge drops below ideal, add more coals.

Serves 20 to 25, or feed your family and freeze the leftovers. Smoked venison is a real treat served along with traditional family favorites during the holidays.

Dinner-on-the-Grill

1 pound venison loin steaks, sliced
Allegro Brand Game Tame Wild Game Marinade (this really gives the venison a different flavor)
various vegetables, cut into chunks and placed on skewers—we like to use potatoes, yellow squash, zucchini, onions, mushrooms, peppers, and tomatoes
Italian dressing

Place steaks in a shallow pan or plastic bag. Marinate in Game Tame for five to eight hours in refrigerator. Drain steaks and grill over charcoal (or broil in your oven) to desired doneness.

For vegetables, place on skewers and brush with Italian dressing. Cook along with venison steaks. Since the steaks are ready so quickly, I find it best to partially cook the vegetables in the microwave before placing on skewers to grill. Then everything is ready simultaneously.

Four servings

Tip: Fresh asparagus cooked quickly in the microwave gives you a green vegetable for a delicious and easy meal.

Venison Kabobs

1 pound venison loin, cut into chunks

Herb Marinade

1/2 cup vegetable oil
1/4 cup lemon juice
1 teaspoon salt
1 teaspoon marjoram
1 teaspoon thyme
1/2 teaspoon pepper
1 clove garlic, minced
1/2 cup chopped onion
1/4 cup snipped fresh parsley

Reserve small amount of marinade to brush on vegetables.

Place venison in non-metal container. Mix herb marinade ingredients with wire whisk and pour over venison. Marinate over night. Drain kabobs and place on skewers alternately with desired vegetables which have been brushed with marinade and grill venison until venison is cooked to desired doneness and vegetables are tender. Vegetables we like to use: cherry tomatoes, potatoes, onions, peppers, zucchini, yellow squash, mushrooms.

Four servings

Tip: If you partially cook veggies in the micro-wave before placing on skewers, everything is done at the same time (particularly potatoes).

Wright Sweet Venison Kabobs

4 to 5 pound venison loin
3 large jars button mushrooms
cherry tomatoes
2 large cans of pineapple
chunks

Marinade

1 cup soy sauce
1 cup brown sugar
1/2 cup olive oil

Cut the venison loin into cubes. Heat the marinade and pour over the venison cubes. Store in the refrigerator for four to six hours. String the pineapple, venison, tomatoes and mushrooms alternately on skewers. Cook on a charcoal or gas grill for about 30 minutes. The kabobs are good served over yellow rice with a side salad.

Eight servings

Burgers with Tomato Topper

1 pound ground venison

Handle gently and make into four patties. Grill until done and serve on warm buns with tomato topper.

Tip: Spray grill top with Pam or brush with oil to prevent burgers from sticking.

Tomato Topper for Venison Burgers

2 tablespoons olive oil
2 teaspoons lemon juice
1 teaspoon dried basil
salt and pepper to taste

Mix ingredients with wire whisk. Pour over sliced tomatoes and sliced red onion and toss. Serve on burgers or as side dish.

Four servings

Venison Burgers with Horseradish Sauce

1 pound ground venison
2 tablespoons steak sauce
1/2 teaspoon garlic salt
1/4 teaspoon pepper

Gently mix ground venison with seasonings. Shape into patties. Be sure burgers are well chilled before cooking.

Lightly oil grill top and grill over medium coals about ten minutes, turning over once. Serve on warm buns with lettuce, tomato, pickles, and horseradish sauce.

Horseradish Sauce

1/2 cup plain yogurt (or sour cream)
1 tablespoon prepared horse-radish
1 teaspoon dijon mustard

Blend yogurt, horseradish, and mustard in small bowl. Use as spread for burgers instead of mayonnaise or mustard.

Four servings

Carolina Style Burgers

1 pound ground venison
1/3 cup uncooked oats
1 tablespoon Worcestershire
sauce

Mix above ingredients lightly and make into four patties. Grill, broil, or pan fry burgers. Do not over cook and turn only once.

About seven minutes is long enough. Serve on buns with Hot Dog/Burger Chili (see recipe), cole slaw, mustard, and onions. Pile condiments high and provide lots of napkins!

Four servings

Tip: Serve with frosty mugs of beer.

Eddie Salter's Venison and Pork Roast

3 pound venison roast
3 pound pork roast
seasonings: garlic, salt and
pepper, Italian dressing, or
other herbs and spices of
your choice

Place venison in heavy duty foil, season, and top with pork roast and season. Wrap in foil and bake or grill until tender and pork is done.

Barbecue Whole Deer

Slow cook in outdoor barbecue pit, basting all day with oil and vinegar. Cook until tender.

Serve plain or use barbecue sauce of your choice.

4

Ground Venison and Cubed Steak

Although there is no reason that venison should not be as tender as the finest cuts of beef, if properly handled and aged, the realities of "hurry up" processing often dictate that such is not the case. One of the easiest answers in such situations is to have most of your deer ground up or made into cubed steak. Also, it is worth noting that portions of the deer which are sometimes overlooked or discarded (such as the neck and ribs) can easily be utilized in ground meat. Ground venison is every bit as versatile as hamburger, lending itself readily to everything from pizza pies to backyard burgers, chili to casseroles. Likewise, cubed steak is surprisingly versatile, lending itself to dishes ranging from Italian specialties to regional American cuisine.

This section offers dozens of dishes featuring ground or cubed meat, and several of them are among our favorites of all the myriad ways to prepare venison. You will find lots of "quick" treats for lunch, and many of them, such as chili, tacos, and sloppy joes, can be prepared in advance and then heated in just a few minutes. For those of you who deal daily with the appetites of youngsters, which can be at once ravenous and highly selective, we suspect that you will find some of the ground meat dishes especially appealing.

Venison Scaloppine

1 tablespoon all-purpose flour
1/2 teaspoon salt
dash pepper
4 venison cubed steaks (about
  one pound)
3 tablespoons canola oil
1/2 medium onion, thinly
  sliced
1 can (16 ounce) tomatoes, cut
  up
1/3 cup red wine
1 can (3 ounce) mushrooms,
  sliced (2/3 cup)
1 tablespoon snipped parsley
1/4 teaspoon garlic salt
1/4 teaspoon dried oregano,
  crushed
hot buttered noodles

Combine flour, salt, and pepper; coat venison steaks lightly with flour mixture. In medium skillet, brown venison slowly in hot oil; remove from skillet. Add onion to skillet; cook until tender. Add cooked venison, tomatoes, wine, mushrooms, snipped parsley, garlic salt and oregano. Cover and simmer 20 to 30 minutes or until venison is tender, stirring occasionally.

Arrange venison and sauce on hot buttered noodles.

Four servings

Venison Piccata

1 pound venison steak cutlets,
  cubed and/or pounded until
  thin - about 1/4 inch
salt and pepper to taste
1/4 - 1/3 cup flour
2 tablespoons olive oil
1 tablespoon margarine
1 clove garlic, minced
1/2 cup water
1/4 cup white or blush wine
1 teaspoon chicken flavored
  bouillon crystals
1 lemon, divided
1 tablespoon parsley

Pound cutlets. On waxed paper sprinkle with salt and pepper and coat with flour.

Quickly brown cutlets in two tablespoons hot olive oil. Remove from pan.

Reduce heat to medium low. Into drippings add one tablespoon margarine (or add to pan earlier if not enough olive oil), water, wine, minced garlic, juice of one-half lemon, and one tablespoon parsley. Scrape to loosen brown bits. Return venison cutlets to skillet, place thin slices of lemon on each cutlet. Cover and simmer ten to fifteen minutes until venison cutlets are tender.

Two or three servings

Tip: Serve with garlic spaghetti and hot, crusty homemade bread.

Oven Swiss Steak

3/4 - 1 pound boneless venison cubed steak
2 tablespoons olive oil
3 tablespoons all-purpose flour
1/2 teaspoon salt
1 can (14 ounces) tomatoes
1/2 cup chopped celery
1/2 cup chopped carrot
2 tablespoons chopped onion
1 teaspoon Worcestershire sauce
1/4 cup shredded cheddar cheese

Cut meat into two portions. Mix flour and salt; dredge meat; set aside remaining flour. Brown venison steaks. Place venison in 11 x 7 baking dish. Blend remaining flour with drippings in skillet. Add remaining ingredients, except cheese, and cook, stirring constantly, until mixture boils. Pour over meat. Cover and bake in 350 degree oven for 1 hour or until meat and vegetables are tender. Sprinkle cheese over meat. Return to oven for a few minutes to melt cheese.
Two servings

Country-Style Venison Steak

1 pound venison cubed steak
2 tablespoons olive oil
1/3 cup flour
salt and pepper to taste
1 medium onion
1 jar (4 ounces) whole mushrooms

Mix flour, salt and pepper. Dredge steak in flour and brown quickly in oil. Place in 8 x 11 casserole dish. Slice onion and cook until tender. Place on top of steak along with drained mushrooms. Add two tablespoons remaining flour to pan drippings. Stir until brown, add one to one and a half cups water and cook until thick. Pour over steaks. Bake covered in a 350 degree oven for one hour or until tender.
Three or four servings

Quick and Easy Venison Stroganoff

1 pound venison cubed steak
2 tablespoons canola oil
3- 6 green onions, chopped
1 clove garlic, minced
1 cup fresh mushrooms, sliced
1 can (10 3/4 ounce) cream of mushroom soup
1/4 - 1/3 cup fat free sour cream
2 tablespoons ketchup
1 teaspoon Worcestershire sauce
1 teaspoon beef bouillon granules
1 package (8 ounce) egg noodles, cooked and drained

Cut venison cubed steak into strips and brown quickly in two tablespoons canola oil in heavy skillet with onions, garlic, and mushrooms. Add soup, ketchup, Worcestershire sauce, bouillon and sour cream. Heat together and serve over cooked, hot noodles.

Three or four servings

Vegetables and Venison in Burgundy Sauce

1/3 cup all-purpose flour
1 teaspoon salt
1/4 teaspoon pepper
1 pound venison cubed steaks
2 tablespoons cooking oil
2 cups chopped vegetables-
  -celery, carrots, fresh mushrooms and onions
1 cup beef broth
1/4 cup burgundy wine
1 garlic clove, minced
1 teaspoon Worcestershire
  sauce

Combine flour, salt and pepper. Cut steaks into serving size pieces; dredge in flour mixture. In a skillet, quickly brown steak in two tablespoons oil. Remove and place in a two quart casserole. Leave only one tablespoon oil in skillet. Add vegetables and sauté lightly. Add beef broth, wine, and Worcestershire sauce and bring to a boil. Pour over steaks. Cover and bake at 350 degrees for one hour or until meat is tender.

Four servings

Tip: Serve over rice, noodles, or potatoes.

Mustard Fried Venison Steak

1 pound venison cubed steak
6 tablespoons canola oil
1/2 cup prepared mustard
  (French's)
2/3 cup flour
1 teaspoon salt

Brush venison cubed steak on both sides with prepared mustard. Place flour and salt in paper bag. Shake to mix. Add one half of steak and shake to flour steaks. Repeat.

Heat six tablespoons oil in non-stick fry pan and add floured steaks. Cook until golden brown. Serve immediately.

Three or four servings

Rice and Venison Casserole

1 pound ground venison
1/2 cup chopped onion
1/2 cup chopped celery
1/2 cup sliced mushrooms
1 clove garlic, minced
1 cup raw rice (regular long
  grain rice)
1 can (10 3/4 ounce) cream of
  mushroom soup
1 can (10 3/4 ounce) consommé
1 can water
1 cup sour cream
1 tablespoon soy sauce
1 teaspoon Worcestershire
  sauce

Brown venison in skillet and place in three quart casserole. Sauté onion, celery, mushrooms, and garlic. Add to casserole. Melt one tablespoon margarine in skillet and brown rice. Add rice and remaining ingredients to casserole. Stir and blend well. Bake uncovered at 350 degrees for one hour or until rice is tender. Stir occasionally.

Six to eight servings

Croquettes

1 pound ground venison, uncooked
1/2 cup onion, finely chopped
1 garlic clove, minced
salt and pepper to taste
2 cups cooked, mashed potatoes (no butter or milk added)
1/4 cup milk
1 egg, beaten
Cracker meal (make by placing
   crackers in blender or processor)

Lightly mix venison, onion, garlic, potatoes, and salt and pepper. Make out into patties. Beat egg and milk in a shallow dish. Dip patties in milk and egg mixture. Roll in cracker meal.

Brown patties in non-stick skillet with enough oil to keep from sticking (two or three table-spoons). Cook over medium heat until done. Serve immediately.

Six to eight servings

Venison Patties with Wine Sauce

1 pound ground venison
1 grated raw potato

Sauce

1 carrot, finely diced
1 small onion, finely chopped
1 garlic clove, minced
3 tablespoons fresh chopped
  parsley
2 tablespoons margarine
1 tablespoon olive oil
1 cup red wine
1/2 cup beef broth
1 tablespoon tomato paste
1 tablespoon cornstarch

Lightly mix venison and potato and make into one-fourth pound patties.

Sauté carrot, onion, garlic, and parsley in margarine and olive oil. Add wine, beef broth, and tomato paste. Simmer ten minutes or until carrot is tender. Dissolve cornstarch in two tablespoons water and add to sauce. Simmer until thickened. Pour sauce over cooked patties.

Four servings

Oven Meat Balls

2 pounds ground venison
1 cup quick or regular oats
  (Not instant)
1 cup soft bread crumbs
1/2 cup milk
1 teaspoon salt

Mix above ingredients and roll into two-inch balls. Roll meatballs in flour and place in a casserole. Pour one envelope dry onion soup mix and one and one-half cups water over meatballs. Bake at 350 degrees for one hour.

Quick and Easy Ground Venison Barbecue Sauce

1 tablespoon margarine
1/2 cup chopped onion
1 cup ketchup
1 tablespoon prepared mustard
1 tablespoon vinegar
juice of one lemon
2 tablespoons brown sugar
1/2 teaspoon salt
1/4 teaspoon pepper
1/4 teaspoon paprika
2 tablespoons Worcestershire
  sauce
hot sauce to taste

In small saucepan sauté onion in margarine. Add remaining ingredients and simmer, covered, fifteen minutes or until sauce is thickened.

In skillet brown one pound ground venison crumbling it with a fork. Drain, if necessary. Add sauce and simmer, covered, for fifteen minutes or until ready to serve.

Four or five servings

Tip: Serve on onion rolls with cole slaw for a quick and easy meal.

Stuffed Cabbage

1 medium head green cabbage
1 can (16 ounce) sauerkraut
1/2 cup white rice
1 pound ground venison
1/2 pound ground pork
1 egg
1/2 teaspoon garlic salt
2 tablespoons oil
1 tablespoon flour

Place cabbage leaves in hot water to get soft while making meat balls.

Lightly mix meats, rice, egg and garlic salt and form into two inch balls and wrap with cabbage leaves. Use toothpicks to secure, if necessary, but if you fold leaves, the toothpicks are not necessary. Place cabbage leaves in dutch oven to cover bottom of pan and to keep balls from sticking. Place meatballs wrapped in cabbage leaves in pan. Cover with a can of sauerkraut; then cover with water. Cook for about four hours at medium heat or until cabbage is very tender.

Then mix two tablespoons oil and one tablespoon flour in skillet.

Cook on medium heat until lightly browned and add one teaspoon paprika. Pour into cabbage rolls and let come to a boil.

Serve immediately with warm rye bread.

Four to six servings

Stuffed Peppers

6 medium green peppers
1 pound ground venison
1/2 cup chopped onion
1 garlic clove, minced
2 cups fresh tomatoes,
    chopped (or a 16 ounce can
    of tomatoes)
1 cup cooked long-grain rice
1/2 teaspoon Italian seasoning
1 teaspoon Worcestershire
    sauce
1 cup cheddar cheese, shred-
    ded

Cut off tops of bell peppers; remove seeds and membrane. Scallop edges if desired. Sprinkle inside of cups with salt and pepper.

Brown venison, onion, and garlic. Stir in tomatoes, cooked rice, and seasonings. Add one half cheese. Stuff peppers and place in baking dish. Top with remaining cheese. Bake at 350 degrees for twenty minutes.

Six servings

*Tip: If you do not like your peppers crisp, precook peppers in
boiling salted water about five minutes and drain well.
This same recipe can be used to stuff tomatoes. I use the pulp
from tomatoes and add a little sugar and basil. Top tomatoes
with buttered bread crumbs. Add water to baking dish.*

Stuffed Zucchini

4 zucchini squash, medium
  size
1/4 pound ground venison
1/2 cup chopped onion
1 garlic clove, minced
1/2 cup Parmesan cheese
1/2 cup bread crumbs
1 egg
1/4 teaspoon thyme
1/4 teaspoon paprika
salt and pepper to taste

Cook zucchini whole in salted water or in microwave. Cut in half lengthwise. Remove meat from shells and mash. Cook ground venison, onion, and garlic. Mix with zucchini meat. Add half cheese, bread crumbs, egg, thyme, paprika, salt and pepper. Fill shells. Sprinkle with rest of cheese and paprika. Bake at 350 degrees for thirty minutes or until hot and golden brown on top.

Six to eight servings

Teresa's Shepherd's Pie

2 cans green beans, drained
1 pound ground venison
1 onion, finely chopped (optional)
1 cup chopped mushrooms
   (optional)
1 large can tomato sauce
1 pound cooked mashed
   potatoes (the REAL thing;
   not instant. Leftovers work
   fine.)
1 cup grated cheddar cheese
salt and pepper to taste

Brown ground venison with onions and mushrooms. Drain, if necessary. Add tomato sauce and seasonings to ground venison.

In a deep baking dish layer green beans, ground venison and tomato sauce mixture; top with mashed potatoes and sprinkle grated cheese on top. Bake at 350 degrees for about thirty minutes or until heated through.

Four to six servings

Tip: Other cooked and chopped vegetables (such as peas, carrots, celery) may be added or substituted for the green beans, onions, and mushrooms. What a terrific way to disguise leftovers!

Mexican Venison Pie

1 pound ground venison
1/2 cup chopped onion
2 teaspoons of packaged taco
  seasoning mix
1 teaspoon cilantro
1/2 cup water
1/2 cup chunky salsa
1 can (8 ounce) refrigerated
  crescent rolls
1 cup crushed corn chips,
  divided
1 can (2 1/2 ounce) sliced
  black olives
1 - 1 1/2 cups sour cream
1 cup shredded cheddar or
Monterey Jack cheese

Brown venison and onion in a large skillet. Stir seasoning mix into water and add to venison along with salsa and cilantro. Simmer while preparing crust. Spread the crescent roll dough in a ten inch pie place to form crust. Be sure to press edges together at seams. Sprinkle one-half cup crushed corn chips over crust. Distribute sliced olives evenly over chips. Spoon venison mixture over olives. Spread sour cream on top (fat free does fine). Cover with shredded cheese and top with remaining chips. Bake at 375 degrees for fifteen to twenty minutes or until crust is golden brown.

Six servings

Texas Hash

3 tablespoons bacon drip
  pings (this adds more flavor
  BUT canola oil can be substituted)
2 onions, chopped
2 green peppers, chopped
1 pound ground venison
1 teaspoon salt
1/4 teaspoon pepper
1/2 cup uncooked rice
1/2 teaspoon chili powder (or
  to taste)
4 cups tomato juice

In skillet sauté onions and peppers in bacon drippings. Add ground venison, salt and pepper and cook until venison is no longer pink. Add rice, chili powder, and tomato juice. Place in casserole and bake uncovered at 350 degrees for about forty five minutes or until rice is tender.

Six servings

Ground Venison Stroganoff

1 pound ground venison
1 medium onion, chopped
1 can (8 ounce) mushrooms, drained
1 can (10 1/2 ounce) cream of chicken soup
1/2 pint sour cream
2 tablespoons parsley

Brown venison and onion and add mushrooms, soup, salt, and pepper. Simmer ten minutes. Stir in sour cream and parsley and heat through. Do not boil. Serve over pasta or rice.

Four servings

Tip: Use this same recipe but marinate chunks or cubes of venison in wine, pickling spices, and rosemary for four to six hours and complete recipe as above.

Eggplant and Ground Venison Casserole

1 pound ground venison
2 tablespoons canola oil
1 medium eggplant
1/3 cup flour
1/4 cup olive oil
 2 cans (8 ounce each) tomato
  sauce
1 teaspoon oregano
1 tablespoon grated Parmesan
  cheese
1 cup grated cheddar cheese
1 teaspoon salt
pepper to taste

Shape venison into thick patties. Season to taste with salt and pepper. Brown in hot canola oil. Slice eggplant into thick slices (skin left on). Season with salt and pepper, coat with flour and brown in olive oil. Place cooked eggplant slices in shallow baking dish. Top each with browned venison patties. Cover with tomato sauce. Sprinkle oregano and Parmesan cheese over all. Top with grated cheddar cheese. Bake at 300 degrees for thirty-five minutes.

Six servings

Family Ground Venison Casserole

1 medium onion, finely chopped
1 tablespoon canola oil
1 pound ground venison
2 1/4 cups cooked rice (3/4 cup raw)
1 large can tomatoes (2 1/2 cups)
3 tablespoons soy sauce
1 tablespoon Worcestershire sauce
1 teaspoon curry powder
1 teaspoon onion salt
1/8 teaspoon pepper
3 strips bacon

Brown ground venison and onion in one tablespoon oil. Mix with cooked rice, tomatoes, and seasonings. Place in one and one-half quart casserole and top with bacon. Bake at 375 degrees until bacon is crisp (about thirty minutes).

Six servings

Cheeseburger Pie

1 pound ground venison
1/2 cup evaporated milk
1/2 cup ketchup
1/3 cup fine dry bread crumbs
1/4 cup chopped onions
1/2 teaspoon dried oregano
salt and pepper to taste
1 cup cheddar cheese, shredded
1 teaspoon Worcestershire sauce
1 8-inch prepared pie shell

Combine ground venison, milk, ketchup, bread crumbs, onion, and oregano. Season to taste with salt and pepper. Prepare pastry to line one 8-inch pie plate (or used prepared shell). Fill with venison mixture. Bake at 350 degrees for thirty five to forty minutes. Toss cheese with Worcestershire sauce; sprinkle on top of pie. Bake ten minutes more. Let stand ten minutes before servings.

Six servings

Onion Rings and Venison Casserole

1 pound ground venison

Brown ground venison and add:

**1/4 teaspoon garlic salt
1 teaspoon oregano
2 small cans tomato sauce
(optional additions: mushrooms, onions, peppers)
8 ounces twist pasta, cooked**

Mix together:

**4 ounces cream cheese
8 ounces sour cream**

Simmer for ten minutes while preparing other ingredients. Cook eight ounces twist pasta.

Layer in an 8 x 12 casserole dish in the following order:

1. Cooked pasta mixed with 1/2 can Durkee's French Fried Onion Rings. Crush onion rings mixed with pasta and reserve others for top.
2. Thin layer of cheese mix.
3. Meat mixture.

Bake at 350 degrees for twenty-five minutes. Top with remainder of can of onion rings and bake about five minutes more or until onions are hot and very golden.

Serve immediately.

Four to six servings

Venison Noodle Casserole

1 pound ground venison
3 cups egg noodles (medium
  size), uncooked
1/4 - 1/2 green bell pepper,
  chopped
3 cups tomato juice
1 1/2 teaspoon celery salt
salt and pepper to taste
1 teaspoon Worcestershire
  sauce
1/2 cup chopped onions
1 can mushroom soup

Brown venison in large skillet. Add salt, pepper, onion, bell pepper, noodles (uncooked), tomato juice, celery salt, and Worcestershire sauce. Bring to a boil and cover. Simmer until noodles are tender. Add mushroom soup, stir and heat through. Serve immediately.

Four to six servings

Layered Casserole

1 pound ground venison
1 medium onion, chopped
1 can (8 ounce) tomato sauce
1/2 teaspoon chili powder (or
  more to taste)
few dashes A-1 sauce
1 teaspoon Worcestershire
  sauce
8 ounce package egg noodles,
  cooked
1 can cream of mushroom
  soup
2 cups grated cheddar cheese

Brown venison and onions. Add tomato sauce, chili powder, A-1, and Worcestershire. Simmer while noodles cook.

Layer in casserole:

ground venison mixture
noodles
cream of mushroom soup,
  undiluted
grated cheddar cheese

Repeat layers.

Bake at 350 degrees for twenty-five to thirty minutes. Serve immediately.

Four to six servings

Delicious Hash Casserole

1 small onion, chopped
1/4 cup canola oil (or less)
1 green bell pepper, chopped
1 pound ground venison
salt and pepper to taste
2 cups mashed potatoes
1 can cream-style yellow corn
2 tablespoons margarine

Cook onion and green pepper in oil until tender. Add venison and seasonings and brown. Place mashed potatoes in casserole. Pour venison mixture over potatoes. Add corn and dot with margarine. Bake at 350 degrees for twenty minutes or until brown.

Six servings

Lee's Tamale Pie

1 1/2 - 2 pounds ground venison
1 package Taco seasoning (use only one-half package for mild)
1 small can (8 ounce) tomato sauce
1 (or 2) small cans sliced black olives (use 2 cans if you really like olives)
1 package (8 ounce) grated cheddar cheese
1 package (8 ounce) grated Monterey Jack or mozzarella cheese
1 package small flour tortillas

Brown venison in skillet; once venison is brown add taco seasoning (amount desired) and tomato sauce.

Place tortilla in bottom of round baking dish. Sprinkle tortilla with meat, cheese, and olives. Repeat this process until you have three or four layers of tortillas, being sure to end with cheese.

Bake in pre-heated 350 oven for thirty minutes or until hot and cheese is slightly brown.

Optional: Onions could be added to ground venison. Add chili powder if you desire it hot. Green chilies or a fresh jalapeno pepper could add more spice.

Four to six servings

Tip: This may be frozen or refrigerated before baking.

Taco Salad

Prepare chili by recipe for Venison Chili Con Carne but do not simmer to thicken. Simmer for only ten to fifteen minutes while you prepare other ingredients as follows:

tortilla chips or corn chips
chopped lettuce
grated cheese
chopped tomato
salsa
sour cream
olives
whatever toppings you prefer

Place chips in plate; top with cheese, chili, and other desired toppings.

Four servings

Mexican Pizzas

1 pound ground venison
2 green onions, chopped
1 can (8 ounce) tomato sauce
salt to taste
1/2 teaspoon chili powder, or
  to taste
1/4 - 1/8 teaspoon ground
  cumin
1/4 - 1/8 teaspoon cilantro
1/4 teaspoon garlic salt
1/2 teaspoon oregano
6 flour tortillas (6 inch size)
vegetable cooking spray
1 cup low fat mozzarella
  cheese (or Monterey Jack)
1/2 cup sliced olives
1 can (16 ounce) no fat refried
  beans
chopped fresh tomatoes
chopped green onion

Heat oven to 400 degrees.

In large non-stick skillet brown ground venison and green onion over medium heat eight to ten minutes or until venison is no longer pink and break up into small crumbles. If there are any drippings, drain well. Add salt, chili powder, cumin, cilantro, garlic salt, and oregano. Stir in tomato sauce. Simmer about ten minutes stirring occasionally.

Warm refried beans in saucepan as meat sauce simmers. Place six tortillas on two baking sheets; lightly spray tortillas with cooking spray. Bake in 400 degree oven for three to five minutes. Place one and a half to two tablespoons refried beans on three tortillas. Cover with other three tortillas and divide venison mixture evenly among three stacks. Sprinkle with shredded cheese and sliced ripe olives.

Return pizzas to oven. Bake about five minutes or until cheese melts. Top with cubed fresh tomatoes and sliced green onions. To serve, cut each pizza into four wedges. *Three servings*

Mexican Pizzas (cont.)

Tip: We are not lovers of hot and spicy foods, so I go very lightly on the herbs and spices. You can certainly adjust them to your tastes and preferences. Also, you can vary the taste with the type of cheese and you can use pita bread for the base. Split them horizontally and omit the cooking spray when baking.

Venison and Pork Pizza

2 ready made pizza crusts (12-inch)
1 jar (16 ounce) pizza sauce
1 pound mozzarella cheese, shredded
1 pound ground venison, cooked and drained and crumbled
1/2 cup onion, chopped and cooked with ground venison
3 slices smoked bacon, cooked and well drained and crumbled
1 cup cooked lean ham, chopped
1 cup venison kielbasa, chopped
1 cup mushrooms
1/2 cup olives (or any other vegetables of your choice)

Place one half of the jar of sauce on each pizza crust, add one half of cheese (one fourth on each pizza), sprinkle with cooked ground venison, crumbled bacon, ham, kielbasa, mushrooms, olives, etc. Divide evenly between pizzas. Top with remainder of cheese. Bake at 450 degrees for twelve to fifteen minutes or until pizza is hot and cheese is golden. Makes two twelve inch pizzas.

Tip: This can be varied by using the toppings you prefer.

Cheeseburger Venison Pizza

1/4 - 1/2 pound ground venison
1/4 cup chopped onion
3 slices bacon
1 pizza kit (we like Contadina)
8 ounces light mozzarella cheese (in addition to cheese in kit)

Brown venison and onion in fry pan. Cook bacon in microwave on paper towels. Place sauce on crust. Top with kit cheese. Spread venison on top. Crumble bacon and distribute evenly. Top with additional eight ounce package of light mozzarella cheese.

Bake at 425 degrees for eight to ten minutes or until crisp and cheese is melted and golden.

Two or three servings

Half-a-Yard Pizza

1 loaf (18 inches long) French
  bread
1 pound ground venison,
  cooked and drained (if necessary)
18 - 20 slices pepperoni
1/2 pound venison kielbasa,
  cooked and sliced
1 can (6 ounce) tomato paste
1/3 cup chopped onion
1/3 cup chopped green pepper
1/4 cup chopped ripe olives
1/2 teaspoon oregano
salt to taste
1 package (8 ounce) sliced
  mozzarella cheese, halved
  diagonally

Cut bread in half lengthwise and set aside. If you prefer, scoop out a little of the bread in order to have more room for the pizza toppings.

Combine remaining ingredients except cheese; stir well. Spread meat mixture evenly on bread halves; place bread on ungreased cookie sheets. Bake at 400 degrees for fifteen minutes. Remove from oven and place cheese over meat mixture. Continue baking until cheese melts.

Four servings

Bean Burritos

1 pound ground venison
1/4 cup onion, finely chopped
1/2 teaspoon garlic salt
1/4 teaspoon chili powder
1/4 teaspoon ground cumin
Increase or decrease these
  to taste:
  1/4 teaspoon oregano
  1/4 teaspoon cilantro
  1/4 teaspoon red pepper (optional)
1 can (8 ounce) tomato sauce
1 can (15 ounce) pinto beans,
  drained and mashed
8 flour tortillas (about 8 inches), warmed
thinly sliced lettuce
chopped tomatoes
sliced green onions
sour cream

In large non-stick skillet brown venison and onion being sure to break up into small crumbles. Sprinkle seasonings over venison. Stir in tomato sauce. Simmer five to ten minutes. Stir in mashed, drained beans and heat through.

To assemble, spoon equal amount of venison mixture in center of each tortilla. Add desired condiments. Fold bottom edge up over filling. Fold right and left sides to center overlapping edges.

Eight servings

Tip: Makes a filling camp lunch which can be cooked in one pan.

Quick and Easy Venison Tacos

1 pound ground venison
1/2 cup chopped onion
1 medium clove garlic, minced
1 can (8 ounce) tomato sauce
1/2 teaspoon chili powder (or
  to taste)
generous dash freshly ground
  black pepper
salt to taste

Heat non-stick skillet over medium high heat. Spray with Pam. Add ground venison, stirring to break up. Add onion and garlic; continue cooking until venison is brown and onion is tender. Mix in tomato sauce, chili powder, salt and pepper. Heat thoroughly.

Spoon venison mixture into prepared taco shells. Top with grated cheese, shredded lettuce, onions, sour cream and salsa (or your desired toppings. Serve hot.

Six servings

Tip: We prefer the soft flour taco shells. Let each person adjust "heat of tacos with salsa, peppers, chili powder, etc.

Venison Quiche

1 unbaked 9-inch pastry shell
1/2 pound ground venison
1/2 cup mayonnaise
1/2 cup milk
2 eggs
1 tablespoon cornstarch
1 1/2 cups shredded cheese
1/3 cup sliced green onions

Brown venison in skillet over medium heat. Drain, if necessary, and set aside. Blend mayonnaise, milk, eggs, and cornstarch until smooth. Stir in venison, cheese, and onion. Turn into pastry shell. Bake at 350 degrees for thirty-five to forty minutes until brown and knife inserted in center comes out clean.

Six servings

Layered Taco Dip

Layer in a 9 x 13 baking dish the following:

1. 1 can refried beans
2. Saute 1 pound ground venison, I large onion, chopped, and chopped venison kielbasa. Drain, if necessary, and place on beans.
3. 1 small can green chilies
4. 1/2 pound grated Monterey Jack cheese
5. 1/2 pound grated cheddar cheese
6. 1 jar (8 ounce) taco sauce

Bake at 350 degrees until bubbly (about thirty to forty minutes).

Top with guacamole, sour cream, and chopped tomatoes. Serve with sturdy tortilla chips.

Eight to ten servings

Spicy Meat Sandwiches

1 pound ground venison
1 pound bulk pork sausage
1 pound Velveeta cheese
3/4 teaspoon oregano
dash garlic powder
dash Tabasco sauce
1 - 1 1/2 loaves party rye bread

Brown one pound ground venison and one pound bulk pork sausage. Be sure to use good quality sausage so that it is not too fat. We like Neese's or Jimmy Dean brands. Pour off grease. Drain well. Stir in one pound Velveeta cheese. Stir to melt cheese. Add 3/4 teaspoon oregano, dash garlic powder, and dash Tabasco sauce. Keep on low heat while spreading on party rye bread. Fast freeze about ten to fifteen minutes. Then throw them all in a freezer bag and back into freezer. Take out as many as you need and place on cookie sheet and bake at 400 degrees until hot and bubbly—about five to eight minutes.

Swedish Meatballs

1 egg, beaten
3/4 cup milk
4 slices day old bread, crumbled
1 teaspoon salt
1/8 teaspoon pepper
1/2 teaspoon nutmeg
1 teaspoon minced onion
1/2 pound ground venison
2 thinly sliced medium onions
1/4 - 1/3 cup canola oil
2 tablespoons flour
1 teaspoon salt
1/8 teaspoon pepper
2 cups milk

Combine egg, milk, and bread; let stand five minutes; with fork, beat until bread is in fine pieces. Stir in next five ingredients. In skillet, sauté sliced onion in oil until golden and tender; set aside on a paper towel.

Drop meat by rounded teaspoons into oil in skillet; brown quickly; remove to one quart casserole. Repeat until all meat is browned. Add oil as needed. Stir flour, salt and pepper into oil in skillet. Add milk slowly. Stir constantly until thickened. Pour over meatballs; top with sautéed onions. Bake covered at 350 degrees until bubbly (about thirty minutes).

Four servings

Etah's Delicious Party Meatballs

1 1/2 pounds ground venison
1/2 cup dry bread crumbs
1/2 cup milk
1 egg, beaten
1/4 cup onion, finely minced
1 1/2 teaspoon salt
1/4 teaspoon pepper
1/4 teaspoon garlic powder or
  1 clove garlic, minced

Mix above ingredients and shape into balls. Place in baking dish and brown in 350 degree oven for thirty minutes.

Heat a jar (10 ounce) red currant jelly and a jar (12 ounce) chili sauce in large skillet. Add meatballs and simmer for thirty minutes. Transfer to chafing dish. Serve hot.

Party Meatballs

2 pounds ground venison
2 eggs
1/2 teaspoon salt
1/4 teaspoon pepper
1 jar (12 ounce) chili sauce
1 teaspoon lemon juice
1 jar (10 ounce) grape jelly

Mix ground venison, eggs, salt and pepper; shape into small balls.

Combine chili sauce, lemon juice, and grape jelly and place in a 9 x 13 x 2 inch baking pan. Add uncooked meatballs and bake, covered, at 350 degrees for one hour. Remove cover and bake an additional thirty minutes. Transfer to chafing dish and serve hot with toothpicks.

Thirty to forty meatballs

Sloppy Joes

1 pound ground venison
1/2 cup chopped onion
1 garlic clove, minced
1/4 cup celery, chopped
1/4 cup bell pepper, chopped
1/4 cup bottled barbecue
  sauce
1/2 cup ketchup
1 1/2 teaspoons dry mustard
1 teaspoon Worcestershire
  sauce
1/4 teaspoon salt
1/8 teaspoon pepper

In non-stick fry pan, brown venison, onion, garlic, celery, and bell pepper. Add all other ingredients and simmer ten minutes. Serve on warm buns.

Four servings

Black Bean Chili

1 pound ground venison
1/2 cup chopped onion
1/2 cup salsa
1 cup chopped venison kielbasa
1 can (28 ounce) tomatoes
  with liquid, chopped
1 can black beans, rinsed and
  drained
1 cup water
2 tablespoons tomato paste
  salt to taste
1/4 teaspoon ground cumin
1/4 teaspoon garlic powder
1 can green chilies (or to
  taste)

In large skillet, brown venison and onion. If necessary, drain. Add salsa. (A cup can be reserved at this point and used for Quesadillas—see recipe). Add kielbasa and remaining ingredients. Simmer until thick (about thirty minutes).

Four servings

Tip: Serve with Quesadillas.

Venison Chili Con Carne

1 pound ground venison
1 medium onion, chopped
1 clove garlic, minced
1 green pepper, chopped (1/2 cup) - optional
1 quart tomatoes, broken up
1/2 cup red wine - optional
1 can (8 ounce) tomato sauce
1 pound can red kidney beans, drained
1 jar mushrooms, drained
1/2 teaspoon salt
1 - 2 teaspoon chili powder (as desired)
1 bay leaf

In large heavy skillet brown venison, onion, garlic and green pepper until meat is lightly browned and vegetables are tender. Drain, if necessary. Stir in tomatoes, wine, tomato sauce, kidney beans, mushrooms, salt, chili powder and bay leaf. Simmer for one hour. Remove bay leaf. Serve with crackers or crusty bread. Pass additional toppings: chopped onion, grated cheese, extra chili powder

Four servings

Tip: Leftover chili and grits make a delicious, hearty breakfast for those early morning hunts.

Wright Swamp Chili

6 pounds ground venison
2 large onions
2 bell peppers
1 stick margarine or butter
1/2 cup ground chili pepper
1 tablespoon oregano
1 teaspoon garlic powder
1 teaspoon red pepper
2 teaspoons salt
1 tablespoon paprika
1 large can stewed tomatoes
2 cans (8 ounce) tomato sauce
3 cans light red kidney beans
4 cups water

Brown venison in a large skillet and drain in a colander. Chop the onions and peppers and sauté until translucent. Mix the venison, onions, peppers and all other ingredients in a large stew pot. Simmer on low for at least thirty minutes. Freezes well. Great for camping, fishing trips, etc.

Twelve servings

Quesadillas

1/2 pound ground venison
1/4 cup chopped onion
1/4 cup salsa

Brown ground venison and onion; add salsa and set aside. (Or reserve one cup from black bean chili recipe).

1 cup shredded Monterey Jack cheese
1/2 cup cheddar cheese, shredded
4 flour tortillas (about 8 inch) additional salsa

Spray tortilla with vegetable cooking spray and place on cookie sheet. Sprinkle half cheese on tortilla; arrange ground venison over cheese. Top with salsa. Cover with another tortilla and lightly spray top with vegetable spray. Repeat for second tortilla on separate cookie sheet. Bake at 400 degrees about ten minutes or until lightly browned. Serve with additional salsa and sour cream.

Two servings

Venison Meat Loaf with Spinach & Cheese Stuffing

Meat Loaf

1 pound ground venison
1 cup soft bread crumbs
1/3 cup milk
1 egg, beaten
1/2 teaspoon salt
1/8 teaspoon pepper

Filling

1 package (10 ounce) frozen chopped spinach, defrosted and WELL drained
1/2 cup shredded part-skim mozzarella cheese
1/3 cup lite ricotta cheese
3 tablespoons grated Parmesan cheese
1 teaspoon Italian seasoning
1/4 teaspoon garlic salt

Topping

1 jar (14 ounce) prepared spaghetti sauce

Combine meat loaf ingredients in large bowl. Mix lightly but thoroughly. Combine filling ingredients in medium bowl; mix well. Set aside.

Place venison mixture on waxed paper and pat into rectangle—making rectangle the width of your loaf pan and about one-half inch thick. Spread filling over venison leaving an inch border around edges. Using the waxed paper to help, start rolling venison and spinach at short end and roll up jelly-roll fashion. Press venison mixture over spinach filling at ends to seal. Place seam side down in loaf pan.

Make indentations in top with finger and spoon spaghetti sauce into indentations and over and around meat loaf.

Bake in a 350 degree oven for one hour and fifteen minutes. Top with additional mozzarella, if desired.

Venison Meat Loaf with Spinach & Cheese Stuffing (cont.)

To serve cut into 1 1/2 inch thick slices.

Four to six servings

Tip: To drain spinach: Place in colander and gently press water out. Then blot with paper towels. Get as much water as possible out so your filling will not be watery. Bake potatoes while meat loaf is cooking. Wash potatoes well. Rub with canola oil and sprinkle with salt. Place on oven rack.

Moist Venison Meat Loaf

2 slices bread, broken fine
1 1/2 cup milk
1/2 cup oats
1 pound ground venison
1/2 teaspoon salt
2 teaspoon dry onion soup
  mix (or more to taste)
1 egg, beaten
2 1/2 cups canned tomatoes

Soak bread in milk; add oats. Combine with venison, salt, dry onion soup mix, and beaten egg. Mix well and place in loaf pan. Pour one can (2 1/2 cups) tomatoes over all. Bake in moderate oven (350 degrees) for seventy minutes or until bubbly and done.

If desired, add 1 tablespoon pimento and 1 tablespoon chopped green pepper for flavor. One small onion, cut fine, may be used instead of dry onion soup mix.

Four to five servings

Tip: Serve with baked potatoes, steamed broccoli, and fruit salad. Leftovers make good sandwiches— and it is not dry!

Meat Loaf

2 eggs, slightly beaten

Add:
1/3 cup ketchup
3/4 cup warm water

Stir in:
1/2 package Lipton's Onion
  Soup
1 1/2 cup soft bread crumbs
2 pounds ground venison

Mix well and place in loaf pan. Bake at 350 degrees for one hour.

Six to eight servings

Onion Burgers with Zippy Basil Mayonnaise

1 pound ground venison
4 teaspoons beefy onion dry
soup mix
1/4 cup water

Zippy Basil Mayonnaise

3 tablespoons mayonnaise
(light does fine)
1 teaspoon dijon-style mus-
tard
1 teaspoon dried basil leaves
1/4 teaspoon dried parsley
leaves
1/2 teaspoon garlic salt
1/4 teaspoon pepper

Place 1/4 cup water and beefy onion soup mix in glass measuring cup, stir well, and microwave for one minute or until onion is cooked. In medium bowl, combine ground venison and soup/water mixture. Mix lightly but thoroughly. Shape into four patties.

Heat large non-stick skillet over medium heat, spray with Pam, and place patties in skillet; cook seven to eight minutes or until done turning only once.

In small bowl combine Zippy Basil Mayonnaise ingredients. Mix well with wire whisk. Use about one tablespoon mayonnaise mixture per burger. Serve burgers on rolls of choice with Zippy Basil Mayonnaise, lettuce, and sliced tomatoes.

Four servings

Tip: These are delicious grilled also.

Chili and Dogs

1 pound ground venison
1 garlic clove, minced
1 cup V-8 juice
1/4 cup ketchup
1 teaspoon prepared mustard
2 teaspoons chili powder (or
  more to taste)
hot pepper sauce to taste
salt and pepper to taste

Brown venison and garlic in large skillet. Add remaining ingredients and simmer uncovered for twenty minutes or until thickened.

Serve over hot dogs on buns. Top with chopped onion and shredded cheese.

Hot Dog/Burger Chili

1 pound ground venison
1/3 cup chopped onion
1 package Sauer's Chili Seasoning (or use your own)
1/3 cup water
1 can (8 ounce) tomato sauce

Brown venison and onion. Add seasoning package (or your own personal choices), water and tomato sauce. Simmer ten to fifteen minutes until thick. Serve with hot dogs or burgers.

Calzone

3/4 - 1 pound ground venison
1/2 cup chopped onion
1/2 cup sliced fresh mushrooms
1 clove garlic, minced
1/4 cup venison kielbasa
1/4 teaspoon Italian seasoning
1/4 teaspoon oregano
1 jar (14 ounce) tomato and
   basil spaghetti sauce
1 package (8 ounce) refrigerator crescent rolls
flour
8 - 10 ounces grated mozzarella cheese

Sauté venison, onion, garlic, and mushrooms until vegetables are tender and venison is
browned. Add venison kielbasa,
1/4 teaspoon oregano, and 1/4
teaspoon Italian seasoning. Simmer to heat kielbasa.

Place two triangles of crescent dough together to form a
rectangle and press edges together to seal. Roll lightly in
flour. In center of rectangle place
two tablespoons venison and
vegetables mixture. Top with two
tablespoons spaghetti sauce and
grated cheese. Fold one edge of
dough over and seal edges together. Repeat procedure. Place
in oven proof dish. Pour remaining sauce over each. If any venison remains, sprinkle it on top of
sauce. Top with cheese.

Bake at 350 degrees for
twenty minutes.

Four servings

Venison Meatball Subs

Meatballs

1 pound ground venison
1/2 cup Parmesan cheese
1/4 cup milk
1 cup soft bread crumbs
1/4 cup finely chopped onions
1 egg, beaten
1/2 teaspoon garlic salt
1/4 teaspoon black pepper
1/4 teaspoon basil
1/4 teaspoon oregano
1 tablespoon parsley
1/4 teaspoon lemon juice

Sauce

2 tablespoons olive oil
1/2 green bell pepper, cut into
  thin strips (optional)
1/2 red onion, cut into thin
  circles and divided
1/2 cup sliced fresh mush-
  rooms
1/4 teaspoon sugar
1 jar (14 ounce) prepared spa-
  ghetti sauce
4 hoagie rolls, split
1 cup shredded part-skim
  mozzarella cheese

For best results when making meatballs, always be gentle and handle as little as possible. Lightly mix above ingredients. Shape into one-inch meatballs and place on cookie sheet. Place in freezer to get meatballs very cold before cooking (about ten minutes). In large non-stick skillet heat two tablespoons olive oil and add onion, mushrooms, and peppers. Sauté until vegetables are tender. Sprinkle 1/4 teaspoon sugar on veggies, stir, and remove from pan. Add meatballs (which have been chilled thoroughly) to pan and sauté until brown and no longer pink in center (about fifteen minutes). Be sure to turn meatballs gently to keep from breaking up. Add spaghetti sauce and vegetables to meatballs and simmer five to eight minutes until all ingredients are hot.

Split hoagie rolls, place on baking sheet, and sprinkle with mozzarella cheese. Place in 400 degree oven until cheese melts (about five minutes).

Venison Meatball Subs (cont.)

Spoon meatballs and sauce on
rolls. Serve immediately.

Four servings

*Tips: To make soft bread crumbs, place torn bread slices in blender
container and blend turning on and off until all bread is fine crumbs.*

*About two slices of bread for one cup soft bread crumbs. Handle
ground venison gently when making meatballs.*

*Thoroughly chill meatballs before cooking to keep meatballs
from falling apart and sticking to pan.*

Spaghetti and Meatballs

Meatballs

1 1/2 pounds ground venison
1/4 pound ground pork
1/2 cup Parmesan cheese
1/2 cup milk
1 cup soft bread crumbs
1/3 cup onion
1 egg, beaten
1/2 teaspoon salt
1/4 teaspoon black pepper
1/8 teaspoon basil
1/8 teaspoon oregano
1 tablespoon parsley
1 clove garlic, minced
1/8 teaspoon EACH cinnamon, allspice, and nutmeg
1/8 teaspoon red pepper
1/4 teaspoon lemon juice

Mix all ingredients and form into one inch balls. Chill well and brown in one-fourth cup olive oil.

Sauce

1 quart tomatoes, slightly chopped
2 cans tomato paste (12 ounces total)
1/2 teaspoon salt
1/4 teaspoon pepper
1/2 teaspoon oregano
1/2 teaspoon basil
1/8 teaspoon red pepper
1 garlic clove, minced

Simmer sauce until thickened. Add drained meatballs and heat through. Serve over cooked spaghetti or pasta of your choice.

Eight servings

Spaghetti Sauce

2 tablespoons canola oil
1 pound ground venison
1 medium onion, chopped
1 large garlic clove, minced
2 stalks celery, chopped
2 carrots, chopped
1 can mushrooms, drained
2 cans tomatoes (28 ounces
   total)
1 can (6 ounce) tomato paste
1/2 cup red wine
1 teaspoon basil, dried
1 teaspoon oregano, dried
1/2 teaspoon black pepper
1/2 teaspoon salt
1 teaspoon parsley, dried
1 bay leaf
1/2 teaspoon paprika
several dashes Worcester-
   shire sauce
Tabasco sauce to taste
1/2 cup Parmesan cheese
1 cup chopped smoked
   sausage, precooked

In dutch oven heat canola oil. Add ground venison, onion, garlic, celery and carrots. Cook until venison is browned and vegetables are tender crisp. Place tomatoes in blender and chop. Add to venison and vegetable mixture. Stir in remaining ingredients except cheese and sausage. Reduce heat and simmer for one to one and a half hours or until thick. Precook smoked sausage and drain on paper towels. Add sausage and cheese last thirty minutes of cooking.

Serve over vermicelli or spaghetti.

Four to six servings

Variations: Add Italian sausage (precooked) instead of smoked sausage. If you like it hot, add a package of pepperoni. If you use Italian sausage, remove casings and brown; drain well before adding to sauce.

Pastichio

1 pound ground venison
1 medium onion, diced
2 tablespoon margarine
salt and pepper to taste
1/2 teaspoon cinnamon
1/4 teaspoon allspice
1/4 cup sherry (optional)
1 pound cooked, drained
  macaroni

Sauce

1 stick butter or margarine
4 tablespoons flour
1 quart milk
6 eggs, beaten
1 - 1 1/2 cups grated Parmesan
  or Romano cheese

Sauté venison and onion in butter until venison loses its red color and onion is translucent. Add salt, pepper, cinnamon, allspice, and sherry. Add cooked macaroni and mix. Put in 9 x 13 baking dish.

Make sauce by melting one stick butter. Add flour. Stir in milk, beaten with eggs. Add cheese. Cook until thick. Pour sauce over macaroni mixture.

Bake at 350 degrees about one hour or until firm and golden brown on top.

Twelve to fifteen servings

Mousaka with Three Vegetables

1 pound zucchini
1 pound potatoes
1 pound eggplant
1 cup olive oil
2 pounds ground venison
1 large onion, finely chopped
1 clove garlic, minced
2 tablespoons butter
3 medium-size tomatoes,
  peeled and chopped (or
  pound can)
2 teaspoon salt (or to taste)
  dash of pepper
2 tablespoon toast crumbs
3 eggs
parsley

Bechamel Sauce

4 tablespoons butter
6 tablespoons flour
1 teaspoon salt
1/4 teaspoon pepper
dash of nutmeg
2 cups milk
1/2 pound cottage cheese
1/2 cup grated Parmesan
  cheese

Cut zucchini, potatoes, and eggplant into 1/3-inch slices. Heat oil and fry slices a few at a time until slightly brown. (Tip: For eggplant, sprinkle with salt and let stand one hour, rinse and fry.)

Sauté venison, onion, and garlic in butter. Add tomatoes, salt and pepper. Cover and cook over low heat thirty minutes. Remove from heat and add toast crumbs, one beaten egg, and chopped parsley.

Prepare Bechamel Sauce. Melt butter over low heat, adding flour, salt and pepper and nutmeg. Stir until blended. Remove from heat and gradually stir in milk and return to heat. Cook, stirring constantly, until thick and smooth. When thick, remove from heat and gradually add two eggs, slightly beaten, stirring constantly. Add cheeses.

Spray a 9 x 13 x 2 baking dish. Layer potatoes, half meat, eggplant, remaining meat, and zucchini. Top with sauce.

Bake in a 350 degree oven for forty five minutes or until golden.

Eight servings

Manicotti

1 pound Italian link sausage,
   sliced thin
1/4 cup water
1 cup chopped onion
1 pound ground venison
2 cans (10 1/2 ounce each)
   tomato puree
1 can (6 ounce) tomato paste
1 teaspoon basil
salt and pepper to taste
1 teaspoon sugar
1 cup water
1 package (8 ounce) manicotti
   shells
1 carton (16 ounce) ricotta
   cheese
1 package (8 ounce) mozz-
   arella cheese, grated
1 package (10 ounce) frozen
   chopped spinach, thawed
   and drained well
1 egg, lightly beaten
2 tablespoons chopped
   parsley
grated Parmesan cheese

Place sliced sausage and 1/4 cup water in skillet, cover and cook for five minutes. Uncover, drain and brown sausage. Drain again on paper towels and set aside.

Brown ground venison and onion in skillet. Stir in tomato puree, tomato paste, basil, salt and pepper, sugar and one cup water. Cover and simmer for thirty minutes. Add sausage to sauce and simmer ten to fifteen minutes more, stirring occasionally.

Cook manicotti shells according to package directions. Combine ricotta, mozzarella cheese, egg, parsley and spinach. Be sure to drain spinach well. I press the spinach into a colander to get excess water out. Stuff mixture into shells. Place shells in 9 x 13 baking dish which has been sprayed with Pam. Spoon sauce over and around shells. Sprinkle with Parmesan cheese. Bake at 375 degrees for thirty minutes or until hot and bubbly.

Eight servings

Spaghetti Pie

6 ounces spaghetti
1 tablespoon margarine
1 egg, well beaten
1/3 cup grated Parmesan
  cheese
1 cup low-fat cottage cheese
1 pound ground venison
1/2 cup chopped onion
1 clove garlic, minced
1/4 cup chopped celery (optional)
1/4 cup chopped green or red
  sweet bell pepper (optional)
1 jar (14 ounce) spaghetti
  sauce (Classico is a favorite)
1/2 cup shredded mozzarella
  cheese

Cook spaghetti according to package directions; drain and place in bowl with margarine, egg and Parmesan cheese; mix well. Spread in a ten-inch pie plate to form a crust. Spread cottage cheese over crust.

In skillet, brown venison, onion, garlic, celery and green pepper. Stir in spaghetti sauce and simmer ten minutes. Pour over cottage cheese.

Bake uncovered at 350 degrees for twenty minutes. Sprinkle cheese on top and return to oven until cheese melts.

Six servings

Lasagna

1 1/2 pounds ground venison
1 cup chopped onion
1 clove garlic, minced
2 tablespoons olive oil
1 can (16 ounce) tomatoes
2 cans (6 ounce each) tomato
  paste
1 cup water
1/2 cup red wine
1 can mushrooms, drained
1 tablespoon chopped parsley
1 teaspoon sugar
1 teaspoon oregano
1 teaspoon basil
1/2 teaspoon pepper
8 ounces Lasagna noodles
1 pound ricotta cheese
1/2 - 1 cup sour cream
8 ounces mozzarella cheese,
  thinly sliced
1 cup grated Parmesan cheese

In large heavy pan, brown venison, onion and garlic in olive oil. Add tomatoes (chopped in blender), tomato paste, water, wine, mushrooms and other seasonings. Simmer uncovered about thirty minutes. Stir occasionally and cook until thickened.

Cook Lasagna as directed and drain. Spray 9 x 13 x 2 baking pan with Pam; add half noodles, layer of sauce, ricotta (mix with sour cream), mozzarella and Parmesan cheese. Repeat layers ending with sauce and Parmesan cheese.

Bake at 350 degrees for forty to fifty minutes until bubbly. Allow to stand ten minutes before serving. Cut in squares to serve.

Ten to twelve servings

Anita's Venison and Broccoli Crescent Roll

1 pound ground venison
9 ounce package frozen chopped broccoli (thawed and drained)
4 ounces low moisture mozzarella cheese, shredded
1/2 cup chopped onions
1/2 cup sour cream
1/4 teaspoon salt
dash pepper
2 packages Pillsbury crescent rolls
1 beaten egg
poppy seeds

Brown venison and drain. Add all ingredients except crescent rolls, egg, and poppy seeds. Separate crescent roll dough into two rectangles containing eight triangles each; place one rectangle into a cookie sheet, press all perforations together, spoon the filling onto the center, place second rectangle on top of the first and pinch the sides together, brush with beaten egg and sprinkle with the poppy seeds. Bake at 350 degrees for eighteen to twenty-two minutes or until deep golden brown.

Six servings

5

Soups and Stews

Deep in December, one of the best ways to remember the hunts from earlier in the year or yesteryears is with a hot, hearty meal featuring soup or stew. Similarly, a savory stew or a bowl of soup is the perfect way to ward off the miseries of a late winter day when cabin fever threatens your sanity.

Most of the recipes in this section are quite easy to prepare, and almost any type of deer meat—from ground venison to the finest steaks—can be used. For the most part, however, we prefer to utilize the less desirable portions in soups and stews. The nature of the cooking process obviates most concerns about dryness or toughness, and the flavors from vegetables and spices meld with those of the meat in a fashion likely to bring tears of sheer joy to the eyes of the outdoor gourmet.

Brenda's Souper Stew

2 pounds venison, cut into chunks
1 can cream of potato soup
1 can cream of mushroom soup
1 can cream of celery soup
1 package dry onion soup mix
1 can water

Place venison chunks in dutch oven. Mix all soups and water and pour over venison. Bring to a boil, reduce heat and simmer until tender (about 1 1/2 - 2 hours).

Serve over rice or pasta.

Six to eight servings

Tips: This stew does well in the crockpot also. Pour soups over venison and cook on low six to eight hours.

After servings as souper stew, add potatoes, carrots and peas to leftovers to camouflage or use as a base for vegetable venison soup.

Hungarian Venison Stew

1 pound venison, cut into one-inch cubes
1/2 teaspoon ground coriander
1/4 teaspoon ground allspice
1 tablespoon Hungarian paprika
1 teaspoon salt
2 tablespoons flour
2 tablespoons canola oil
1 large onion, sliced
1 green bell pepper, cut into strips
1 garlic clove, minced
1 cup red wine
1 can (16 ounce) whole tomatoes
1 can (11 ounce) beef broth
1 tablespoon parsley
2 large potatoes, peeled and cut into chunks

Combine coriander, allspice and paprika. Mix salt and flour together. Dip venison in spice mixture and then flour. Heat two tablespoons canola oil and brown venison. Stir onion, bell pepper and garlic into venison. Sauté until tender crisp. Add wine, tomatoes, beef broth and parsley. Bring to a boil. Reduce heat and simmer about one hour or until venison is almost tender. Add potatoes to stew and continue to simmer thirty to forty minutes or until potatoes are done and venison is tender.

Six servings

Venison Stroganoff Stew

2 pounds boneless venison
  roast, cut into chunks
1/3 cup margarine
1 large onion, chopped
1 clove garlic, minced
1 tablespoon paprika
1/4 teaspoon red pepper
1 bay leaf
salt to taste
1/2 cup water
1/2 cup red wine
2 tablespoons flour
1 cup sour cream

Melt margarine in dutch oven and sauté onion and garlic until tender. Remove and set aside. Brown venison in dutch oven. Return onion and garlic. Add paprika, red pepper, bay leaf, salt, water and wine. Simmer, covered, one and one-half to two hours or until venison is tender. Add water if necessary. Remove bay leaf. Stir flour into sour cream; add to venison stirring until smooth and thickened. Do not boil.

Serve over pasta—garlic spaghetti or buttered poppy seed noodles.

Six servings

Ginger Ale Stew

2 pounds venison roast, cut
into chunks
1 can mushroom soup, und-
iluted
1/2 envelope dry beefy onion
soup mix
1 can whole pearl onion,
drained
1 can whole button mush-
rooms, drained
1 cup chopped celery
1 cup chopped carrots
1 teaspoon dried parsley
2 cups ginger ale

Mix all ingredients well and place in sprayed casserole dish. Bake uncovered, at 325 degrees for two and a half to three hours or until venison and vegetables are tender. Serve with rice or pasta.

Six servings

Tip: This stew could be prepared in a crockpot. Cook on low six to eight hours.

Sherry Stew

3 pounds venison, cut into
  small chunks
3/4 cup sherry wine
1 clove garlic, minced
2 stalks celery, finely chopped
2 cans golden mushroom
  soup, undiluted
1/2 - 1 package dry onion soup
  mix (according to taste)

Place venison in roasting pan. Add remaining ingredients and mix well. Bake, covered, at 325 degrees for three hours or until tender. Delicious with noodles or rice.

Six to eight servings

Tip: This can also be cooked in a crockpot for six to eight hours.

Red Wine Stew

2 pounds venison, cut into
  one inch cubes
1 teaspoon black pepper (or to
  taste)
1/4 cup flour
1/4 cup canola oil
1 large onion, chopped
1 cup fresh mushrooms,
  sliced
3 medium carrots, thinly sliced
2 stalks celery, thinly sliced
1 cup dry red wine
1/2 cup beef stock
1 bay leaf
1 teaspoon thyme
salt to taste

Mix pepper and flour and dredge venison cubes. Shake off excess flour. Heat 1/4 cup canola oil in dutch oven. Brown venison cubes and remove cubes when browned. Repeat until all venison is browned. Sauté onion, mushrooms, carrots, and celery until tender crisp. Return venison to dutch oven and stir in red wine, stock, bay leaf and thyme. Bring to a boil; reduce heat and simmer about two hours or until venison is tender. Season with salt and pepper if desired.

Six to eight servings

Thirty-Minute Stew

1 pound ground venison
1 cup chopped onion
1 clove garlic, minced
2 cups sliced carrots
1 cup sliced fresh mushrooms
1 cup chopped green bell pepper
2 stalks celery, sliced
1 can (16 ounce) cut green
  beans, drained
1 can (16 ounce) corn, drained
1 can (16 ounce) lima beans,
  drained
1 can (46 ounce) tomato juice
2 teaspoons sugar
1 teaspoon dried basil
1 tablespoon parsley
salt and pepper to taste

Brown ground venison, onion, and garlic in large dutch oven sprayed with Pam. Add remaining ingredients and bring to a boil. Reduce heat and simmer, covered, thirty minutes. Stir occasionally. Adjust seasonings and serve hot. Leftovers may be frozen.

Six to eight servings

Cherry Venison Stew

1/4 cup canola oil
1 cup all-purpose flour
1 teaspoon salt
1 teaspoon pepper
2 pounds venison, cut into
  two-inch cubes
1 can (12 ounce) cola
1 small bottle maraschino
  cherry juice (reserve cherries
  and cut in half)
2 cups chopped pecans
hot cooked noodles

Heat oil in skillet. Mix flour, salt and pepper. Toss venison cubes with flour (a paper bag works well). Brown venison in oil. Remove from skillet and drop in saucepan in which cola and cherry juice are boiling. Reduce heat to low and cook one and a half hours (or until tender). Stir occasionally. Add cherries and nuts. Simmer additional thirty minutes or until meat is tender and gravy is thick. Serve over hot cooked noodles.

Six servings

Tasty Venison and Onion Stew

2 pounds venison, cut into
  small pieces
2 tablespoons canola oil
1 garlic clove, minced
2 medium onions, chopped
1 bay leaf
1 tablespoon dried parsley
salt and pepper to taste
3-5 medium carrots, sliced
3-5 medium potatoes, diced
3 stalks celery, sliced
1 package (10 ounce) frozen
  peas, defrosted

Heat oil in large skillet. Brown venison in oil with onion and garlic. Add salt, pepper, bay leaf, parsley and water to cover and simmer forty five minutes. Add water as needed. Stir often. Allow water to almost cook away before adding more. Add potatoes, carrots and celery and enough water to almost cover. Cover and cook until vegetables are almost tender. Add peas and cook until venison and vegetables are tender.

Dissolve two tablespoons cornstarch in one-half cup cold water and add to stew. Simmer until thickened and starchy taste is gone. Adjust seasonings. Garnish with parsley. Serve with hot homemade bread for a hearty meal.

Six to eight servings

Venison Brunswick Stew

3 pounds venison, cut into
  one-inch cubes
1 large onion, chopped
1 large potato, chopped
2 stalks celery, chopped
1 large can tomatoes, chopped
1 tablespoon Worcestershire
  sauce
1 package (10 ounce) frozen
green lima beans
1 package (10 ounce) frozen
  corn
1 teaspoon salt
1 tablespoon sugar
hot pepper sauce to taste

In large dutch oven brown venison in two tablespoons canola oil. Add chopped onions and sauté. Add potato, celery, tomatoes, Worcestershire sauce and seasonings. Cover and cook for one hour. Check for tenderness. Continue to cook until tender. Add frozen vegetables and cook until they are tender. Taste and adjust seasonings.

Serve over rice.

Six servings

Layered Oven Stew

1 pound venison, cut into bite-size pieces
1 onion, chopped
2 tablespoons flour
salt and pepper to taste
2 stalks celery, sliced
3-4 carrots, sliced
4-5 potatoes, peeled and chopped
1 can sliced mushrooms
1 can (8 ounce) tomato sauce
1 can (10 ounce) cream of mushroom soup
1/2 soup can water
2 tablespoons parsley flakes

Spread venison cubes in 9 x 13 pan. Top with onion. Sprinkle with flour, salt and pepper. Top with celery, carrots, potatoes and mushrooms. Mix tomato sauce, soup and water and pour over all ingredients. Sprinkle with parsley. Cover with foil. Bake at 325 degrees for two and one-half hours or until venison and vegetables are tender.

Six servings

Meatball Stew

1 pound ground venison
1/2 cup soft bread crumbs
1/2 teaspoon dried basil
1 teaspoon dried parsley
1 egg
1 garlic clove, minced
2 tablespoons canola oil
1 can (10 ounce) French onion
  soup
1/4 cup water
2 medium potatoes, peeled
  and quartered
2-3 medium carrots, cut into
  one-inch chunks
1/2 cup celery, chopped
1 medium parsnip, cut into
one-inch chunks

In medium bowl, combine venison, bread crumbs, herbs, egg and garlic. Mix thoroughly but gently. Don't over mix. Shape into meatballs—about twenty.

In ten-inch skillet over medium heat, in hot oil, cook meatballs until browned on all sides. Drain.

Stir soup and water into skillet. Add vegetables. Heat to boiling. Reduce heat to low and simmer thirty minutes or until vegetables are tender. Add more water if needed. Add meatballs to reheat and serve immediately.

Four servings

Venison and Beer Stew

1 pound ground venison
1/2 pound pork sausage
1 egg
1/4 cup finely chopped onion
1 teaspoon salt
1/4 teaspoon pepper
2 tablespoon flour
1 bottle (12 ounces) beer
1 can (8 ounce) tomato sauce
1 cup ripe olives, sliced

Mix together the venison and sausage, egg, onion, salt and pepper. Gently shape into one-inch balls. Brown balls slowly in a hot fry pan. If you do not use pork, you will need to add oil. Set aside meatballs as browned.

Pour off all fat but two tablespoons; sprinkle in the flour and stir until browned. Stir in beer and tomato sauce and cook until sauce is thickened. Return meatballs to sauce and add olives.

Serve with hot homemade bread.

Four to five servings

Tip: Venison sausage can be used but the fat from pork adds a lot of flavor to the sauce.

Italian Soup

1/2 pound ground venison
1/4 cup chopped onion
1 can (14 ounce) Italian stewed
tomatoes
1 can (16 ounce) peeled tomatoes, chopped
1 can (10 1/2 ounce) double
rich beef broth
1 can (8 ounce) mixed vegetables, drained
1/2 cup canned kidney beans,
drained
5 ounce package frozen
chopped spinach, defrosted
1 teaspoon Italian seasoning
1/4 teaspoon garlic salt
1 teaspoon parsley
1/4 teaspoon pepper
1/2 cup uncooked macaroni
noodles

In a large saucepan or dutch oven brown venison and onion. Add tomatoes, broth, vegetables, and seasonings. Bring to a boil; add noodles. Reduce heat to medium and cook ten to fifteen minutes or until macaroni noodles are done.

Four to six servings

Venison and Noodle Soup

1 pound venison, cut into one-inch cubes
2 tablespoon canola oil
1 can (14 1/2 ounce) tomatoes, cut up
1 can (8 ounce) tomato sauce
1 tablespoon plus 1 teaspoon beef bouillon granules
1/4 teaspoon black pepper
2 teaspoons dried basil, crushed
1/2 teaspoon dried marjoram, crushed
2 bay leaves
5 cups water
1 package (16 ounce) frozen mixed vegetables
2 cups uncooked medium noodles

Brown venison in oil in dutch oven. Drain if necessary. Stir in tomatoes, tomato sauce, bouillon, black pepper, basil, marjoram, bay leaves and water. Bring to a boil, reduce heat and simmer, covered, for one hour. Add vegetables and noodles. Simmer, covered, for ten to twenty additional minutes or until vegetables and noodles are done. Remove bay leaves.

Eight to ten servings

Tip: Soup may be prepared in crockpot. Stir in noodles during final thirty to forty minutes of cooking at high setting.

Tex-Mex Cabbage-Venison Soup

1 tablespoon canola oil
1 pound ground venison
1 medium onion, chopped
2 1/2 cups chopped cabbage
  (about 1/2 small head)
1 can (16 ounce) kidney
  beans, undrained
2 cans tomato sauce
1 can (14 ounce) beef broth
1/4 cup mild salsa
1/4 - 1/2 teaspoon cumin
1/2 teaspoon salt
1/2 teaspoon cilantro
Optional toppings: sour
  cream, salsa, grated cheese
  and chopped onion

In large saucepan or dutch oven brown venison with onion in one tablespoon canola oil. Add remaining ingredients. Bring to a boil. Reduce heat and simmer forty-five minutes, stirring occasionally.

Top with a dollop of sour cream and extra salsa. Grated cheese and chopped onions may be added also.

Six to eight servings

Barley Venison Soup

1 cup fine barley, rinsed and
  drained
1 small onion
4 cups beef broth
3 cups frozen mixed vegetables, thawed
1 can (46 ounce) tomato juice
3 or 4 cups leftover venison
  stew
1 teaspoon sugar
salt and pepper to taste

Bring broth to a boil and add washed barley, chopped onion and frozen vegetables. Cook on low about forty minutes until barley and vegetables are done. Add tomato juice and leftover stew and seasonings. Simmer until hot.

Serve with hot homemade corn bread.

Six servings

Ten Bean Soup

1 pound package King's 10
  Bean Soup Mix (or other
  bean soup mixes)
1 cup chopped lean ham (or
  ham hock)
1 can (10 ounce) beer
2 cups water
1 quart canned tomatoes,
  coarsely chopped
1 onion, chopped
1 cup chopped celery
1 clove garlic, minced
1/4 cup lemon juice
1 bay leaf
1 teaspoon salt
1/4 teaspoon pepper
1 cup chopped smoked ven-
  ison sausage or kielbasa

Rinse beans. Combine beans and six cups water and bring to a boil. Boil two minutes. Remove from heat; cover and let stand one hour. Drain beans in colander and rinse.

Combine beans, tomatoes, water, onion, celery, garlic, lemon juice, bay leaf, salt and pepper, and chopped ham in dutch oven. Simmer covered for about one and a half hours or until beans are almost tender. Add smoked venison sausage and cook fifteen to thirty minutes or until beans are tender. Discard bay leaf. Adjust salt and pepper if needed.

Ten to twelve servings

Bean and Barley Soup

3/4 cup dried lima beans
1/4 cup barley
2 quarts water
1 cup chopped ham or a ham hock
1 onion, chopped
1 carrot, chopped
1 teaspoon salt
1/2 teaspoon garlic salt
pepper to taste
1 pound venison, cut into one-inch cubes
1 pint tomato juice

Rinse beans and barley thoroughly. Bring water to a boil in a four quart saucepan. Add venison, ham or hock, and beans. Simmer for several minutes. Skim top off soup. Add barley, onion, and carrot. Add tomato juice. Simmer covered for two and a half to three hours. Cut any meat from bone; discard any bones. Adjust seasonings.

Eight servings

Tip: May be cooked in oven at 325 degrees for two and a half hours.

Wild Rice Soup

1 cup chopped or cubed cooked venison
3 tablespoons margarine
3 tablespoons flour
salt and pepper to taste
1/2 cup chopped celery
1/2 - 3/4 cup onion, chopped
1 can (10 3/4 ounce) beef broth
2 cups milk
1 cup cooked wild rice

Melt margarine in saucepan. Sauté onions and celery until tender crisp. Stir in flour, salt and pepper. Add beef broth and milk. Stir until thickened. Add wild rice and venison.

Four servings

Black Eyed Pea Soup

2 cups dried black eyed peas
4 cups water
**2 cans (14 ounce each) chick-
en broth**
1 cup water
**1 cup venison kielbasa,
chopped finely**
2 cups carrots, sliced
1 cup celery, sliced
1/2 cup chopped onion
1 garlic clove, minced
1 teaspoon dried thyme
1/2 teaspoon black pepper
1/4 teaspoon red pepper
1 tablespoon lemon juice

In large dutch oven bring four cups water and black eyed peas to boil. Boil uncovered for ten minutes. Drain and rinse. Return peas to dutch oven. Add remaining ingredients except lemon juice. Bring to a boil. Reduce heat and simmer, covered, one hour or until peas are tender. Stir in lemon juice and adjust seasonings.

Six servings

Tip: This soup also can be prepared in a crockpot. Combine drained peas (boiled ten minutes) and all other ingredients except lemon juice. Cook on low about eleven hours or high five to six hours. Stir in lemon juice and taste to adjust seasonings.

Vegetable and Venison Soup

1 medium onion, chopped
1 garlic clove, minced
4 carrots, chopped
2-3 potatoes, chopped
2 stalks celery
1 zucchini, chopped
1 yellow squash, chopped
1-2 cups chopped and cooked
   venison (this could be from a
   leftover roast or steak or
   from the Triple Batch Roast)
2 - 3 cans beef broth (or chick-
   en broth)
salt and pepper to taste
1 bay leaf
1 tablespoon dried parsley
1/2 teaspoon Italian seasoning

In a large dutch oven combine all ingredients and bring to a boil. Reduce heat. Simmer, covered, for one hour or until vegetables are tender. Remove bay leaf. Serve hot and top with Parmesan cheese.

Eight to ten servings

Black Bean Soup

2 cups black beans, cleaned,
  rinsed, and soaked
6 cups cold water
2 cups chicken broth
1 medium onion, chopped
1 garlic clove, minced
2 tablespoons margarine
2 bay leaves
2 tablespoons parsley
1 ham hock
1 cup venison kielbasa or
  smoked venison sausage,
  finely chopped
1/3 cup sherry (optional)
salt and pepper to taste

Soak beans. Drain. Fill dutch oven with ham hock, beans, water and broth. Cook on low until beans are tender. Sauté garlic, onion, and parsley in margarine and add to soup along with all other ingredients except sherry. Continue cooking over low heat until soft (about three hours). Add small amount of water if becomes too thick. Remove bay leaves and hock and chop ham into small pieces. Return to kettle with sherry. Garnish with shredded cheddar cheese, sour cream, and chopped onion.

Six servings

Pinto and Navy Bean Soup

1/2 pound pinto beans
1/2 pound navy beans
4 garlic cloves, minced
2 - 4 large carrots, chopped
2 tablespoons oil
2 tablespoons flour
paprika
3/4 cup shell macaroni,
cooked
1 1/2 cups smoked venison
   sausage or venison kielbasa,
   sliced
salt and pepper to taste

Rinse beans and discard stones, bad beans, etc. Soak over night in water.

In large dutch oven place drained beans, chopped garlic, chopped carrots, and water to cover. Bring to a boil, reduce heat and simmer until beans are done (about one and a half hours). Add water if necessary; do not let beans get too dry.

In a skillet make a roux out of two tablespoon oil and two tablespoons flour. Stir constantly until light brown and smooth. Add paprika to give a deep red color. Add roux to beans along with cooked macaroni, venison kielbasa, and seasonings. Simmer fifteen to twenty minutes or until thickened and sausage heated through.

Six to eight servings

Lima Bean Chowder

2 strips bacon, chopped
1/2 cup onion, chopped
1 garlic clove, minced
1 can (16 ounce) chicken broth
1/2 cup carrots, cubed
1 cup potatoes, cubed
1 cup mushrooms, sliced
1 package (10 ounce) frozen
 tiny green lima beans
several dashes nutmeg
1/2 teaspoon dill weed
1 small can evaporated milk
1 cup venison kielbasa,
 chopped
salt and pepper to taste
paprika

Cook bacon in a large, heavy skillet. Sauté onion and garlic in bacon drippings. In a large saucepan place the bacon, onion, garlic, broth, carrots, potatoes, mushrooms, green lima beans, nutmeg and dill weed. Cover and simmer until limas and vegetables are tender. Stir in kielbasa, evaporated milk, and salt and pepper to taste. Simmer to heat through and serve hot with a dash of paprika on each serving.

Four servings

Split Pea Soup

1 cup chopped cooked ham
1 cup venison kielbasa,
 chopped
1/2 pound dried split green
 peas
2 carrots, chopped
2 potatoes, peeled and
 chopped
1 small onion, chopped
salt and pepper to taste

In a large kettle combine ham, venison kielbasa, peas, carrots, potatoes, onion, 6 cups water, and salt and pepper. Bring to a boil. Reduce heat and simmer covered one hour or until peas are tender. With a potato masher, mash vegetables right in kettle. Adjust seasonings and simmer uncovered about 15 minutes for a thick soup.

Six servings

Tip: Serve with steamed pumpernickel bread.

Cabbage Soup with Venison Meatballs

1 pound ground venison
1 egg
1/2 cup seasoned bread
  crumbs
1 tablespoon dried parsley
  flakes
1 tablespoons canola oil
1 onion, chopped (1 cup)
1 clove garlic, minced
1 cup sliced carrots
1 cup sliced celery
2 potatoes, peeled and
  chopped (about two cups)
4 cups shredded cabbage
2 cans (14 ounce) double
  strength beef broth
2 cans water
1 bay leaf
1/2 teaspoon thyme
salt and pepper to taste

Combine ground venison, egg, bread crumbs and parsley. Shape into small teaspoon-size balls and place in refrigerator for thirty minutes or longer.

In large soup pot or dutch oven heat two tablespoons canola oil and brown meatballs in single layers. Remove and set aside.

Add onion and garlic to pot. Sauté until tender. Add carrots, celery, potatoes, cabbage, broth, water, bay leaf, and thyme. Bring to boil. Simmer twenty minutes. Add meatballs. Simmer ten minutes. Adjust seasonings and add salt, more parsley, if desired, and pepper. Simmer until all the vegetables are soft.

Serve with hot corn bread.

Six servings

Tip: Meatballs stay together better
if chilled well before browning.

Paella

1 whole chicken, cooked and cut into large chunks
1 cup smoked venison sausage or kielbasa, cut into bite-size pieces
2 cups seafood, such as shrimp, crab, scallops, fish—uncooked
1 bell pepper, cut into strips
1 onion, chopped
2 garlic cloves, minced
1 cup long grain rice (uncooked)
1/4 cup olive oil
2 cans chicken broth—about 3 cups (or use broth from cooking chicken. Be sure to chill and remove fat. Add celery, onion, and carrots to chicken as it cooks for a more flavorful broth.)
salt and pepper to taste
1/4 teaspoon saffron
Parmesan cheese

In a skillet sauté the bell pepper strips in olive oil until tender crisp. Remove and place on paper towels to drain. Sauté the onion, garlic and sausage until onion is tender.

Pour the broth into a large dutch oven. Add chicken, onions, garlic and sausage. Bring to a boil. Add rice, reduce heat, cover tightly, and simmer for about twenty minutes or until rice is tender. Add chosen seafood, saffron, salt and pepper and simmer until seafood is cooked.

Place bell pepper on top of paella and garnish with Parmesan cheese. Serve with green salad.

Four to six servings

6

Sausage, Jerky, & Little-Used Parts

Too often, portions of a deer which are perfectly palatable are thrown away. It is troubling to see hunters or processors discard organ meats, and even more so to see ribs, flank, and neck go to waste. Most of the recipes which follow focus on utilizing these overlooked portions, but we also include several preparations for jerky and a number of ways to use the various types of venison sausage. Incidentally, little used parts are ideal for use in making sausage or ground meat, and the truly caring hunter will find a way to use all of the meat he kills. These recipes open up avenues to good feelings in that regard as well as to plenty of good tastes.

Ribs in Beer

4 - 5 pounds venison ribs
3 - 4 beers (12 ounce) or
  enough to cover ribs
2 onions
lots of black pepper
salt to taste

Place ribs in dutch oven. Quarter onions and add to dutch oven. Cover with beer. Add black pepper (lots) and salt to taste. Simmer until tender. Remove from dutch oven and drain well. Grill (or broil) and baste with barbecue sauce of your choice.

Four or five servings

Stove Top Ribs

3 pounds venison short ribs
2 tablespoons canola oil
1/4 cup water
1 small can tomato sauce
1 cup ketchup
3/4 cup brown sugar, firmly
  packed
1/2 cup vinegar
2 tablespoons prepared
  mustard
1/2 cup chopped onion
1 garlic clove, minced
salt and pepper to taste

In a large skillet, brown ribs on all sides in two tablespoons canola oil. Add one-fourth cup water, cover, and cook on low about one hour. Drain off drippings.

Combine all remaining ingredients and pour over ribs. Cover tightly and simmer one to one and a half hours or under tender.

Four to six servings

Oven Baked Ribs

4 - 5 pounds venison ribs
1 cup strong coffee
1 tablespoon light brown
  sugar
1 tablespoon Worcestershire
  sauce
1 tablespoon Dale's steak
  seasoning

Place ribs in bottom of roasting pan. Combine coffee and remaining ingredients. Pour over ribs. Cover and bake in 350 degree oven for two hours or until ribs are tender. Cover may be removed during last twenty minutes to brown ribs. Add more coffee or water if ribs become dry.

Three to four servings

Tip: This method may also be used with your favorite barbecue sauce. Just be sure the sauce does not stick and burn during baking.

Kielbasa Chicken

4 boneless chicken breasts
1/2 pound venison kielbasa,
  chopped
1 can sliced mushrooms,
  drained well
1/2 cup sour cream (fat free)
1 can (10 3/4 ounce) condensed cream of mushroom
  soup

Flatten each breast with mallet. Place very finely chopped venison kielbasa and sliced mushrooms on chicken breast. Roll breast and use toothpicks to secure. Place in a shallow casserole. Sprinkle remainder of kielbasa and mushrooms over chicken. Combine sour cream and soup and pour over chicken. Bake uncovered at 300 degrees for one and a half to two hours or until tender. The kielbasa gives chicken a pleasantly different flavor.

Four servings

Chicken and Venison Sausage Bog

1 medium chicken fryer, cut up
1 medium onion
2 - 3 stalks celery
salt and pepper to taste
1/2 - 3/4 pound smoked venison sausage (or kielbasa)
1 cup uncooked long-grain rice

Sprinkle chicken pieces with salt and place in dutch oven with enough cold water to completely cover. Add onion, celery and pepper. Simmer until chicken is tender, about forty five minutes. Remove chicken, saving broth. Let chicken cool and then remove and discard skin and remove meat from bone. Cool broth and skim off fat. Measure broth back into pot. I do not drain onion and celery. Add water if necessary to make four cups liquid. Return chicken to pot. Cut smoked sausage into one-fourth inch slices. Add to pot along with rice. Stir and add salt and pepper to taste. Bring to boil, reduce heat, cover and cook about thirty minutes or until most of broth is absorbed into rice.

Four to six servings

Guatemalan Rice

1 red bell pepper, chopped
1 yellow pepper, chopped
1 green pepper, chopped
1 onion, chopped
2 cloves garlic, minced
1 cup venison kielbasa,
  chopped
3 cups white long-grain rice
5 cups water
8 chicken bouillon cubes
1/3 cup olive oil
1 cup frozen green peas
salt and pepper to taste

Sauté peas, garlic, onions, and peppers in olive oil. Add venison kielbasa, rice, chicken cubes, salt and pepper, and water.

Simmer until rice is tender and slightly moist. Delicious served with barbecued chicken.

Twenty servings

Rice with Two Sausages

1/2 cup long-grain rice
2 cans chicken broth (or 4 1/2 cups)
2 tablespoons margarine
2 stalks celery, finely chopped
1/2 cup onion, finely chopped
1/2 cup bell pepper, finely chopped
1/2 cup slivered almonds
1/2 pound venison bulk sausage
1/2 pound venison kielbasa, finely chopped

Cook rice in broth for ten minutes. Sauté the celery, onion, bell pepper, and almonds in margarine and add to rice and broth mixture. Cook venison bulk sausage; drain and crumble. Mix sausage and finely chopped venison kielbasa into rice mixture. Bake in casserole dish at 350 degrees for one hour.

Six to eight servings

Venison Steak and Kidney Pie

1 cup kidney (venison or beef),
   cooked and cut into bite-size
   pieces
2 cups venison steak, cooked
   and cut into bite-size pieces
3 tablespoons margarine
1/2 cup chopped onion
1 cup fresh mushrooms,
   sliced
3 cups beef broth
3 tablespoons flour
salt and pepper to taste
dash ground cloves
dash marjoram
1 tablespoon Worcestershire
   sauce
Pastry for 10-inch top crust

To prepare kidney: Clean and split kidney; remove fat and large tubes. Soak in salted water for one hour. Dry and cut into one-fourth inch slices. Simmer in beef bouillon or broth until tender (about one hour).

Cut venison steak into bite-size pieces. This is a great way to use leftovers or re-cycle. Triple Batch Roast could also be used here. Be sure you are using tender venison steak.

Sauté onions and mushrooms in margarine (or cook in microwave).

Place cooked kidney, cooked venison steak, cooked onions, and mushrooms in shallow baking dish. Mix broth, flour, salt, pepper, Worcestershire sauce, cloves, and marjoram. Pour broth over steak and kidney.

Cover with pastry. Make vents in pastry to allow steam to escape. Bake at 375 degrees for thirty to forty-five minutes or until crust is golden.

Eight servings

Pasta Nest with Kidneys

8 ounces noodles or pasta
2 tablespoons margarine
4 - 5 slices bacon, diced
8 - 10 pearl onions
1 cup fresh mushrooms
2 - 3 deer kidneys, skinned
  and halved or quartered
salt and pepper to taste

Cook pasta until just tender. Drain carefully and transfer to a buttered one quart ring mold. Dot with two tablespoons margarine and bake in a 375 degree oven for fifteen minutes.

Place diced bacon in a skillet and fry onions whole with the bacon. Add the kidneys and mushrooms to the pan and fry for a few minutes, turning frequently. Season to taste. Continue to cook over moderate heat for five minutes.

Remove ring mold from oven and turn out onto a serving plate.

Arrange the kidney mixture in the center and serve hot.

Two to three servings

Kidneys and Scrambled Eggs

2 deer kidneys
3 tablespoons margarine
1 clove garlic, minced
salt and pepper to taste
4 eggs, lightly beaten
1 tablespoon water
1 tablespoon margarine, cut
  into pieces
dash of nutmeg
1 tablespoon cream

Cut kidneys in half and remove any white parts from the center. Melt three tablespoons margarine in a skillet. Brown kidneys for two minutes on each side over a low heat. Add garlic. Season with salt and pepper. Cover and cook four to five minutes over very low heat. Remove from heat and keep warm.

Break eggs into a bowl. Add one tablespoon water and whisk eggs briefly. Add margarine cut into pieces and nutmeg. Season with salt and pepper. Scramble eggs in a non-stick pan, stirring constantly but gently, until eggs thicken. Add cream and additional margarine in small pieces if desired. Stir for another minute.

Pour eggs into hot serving dish and top with kidney halves. Serve immediately.

Two servings

Broiled Kidneys

3 deer kidneys
3 tablespoons olive oil
salt and pepper to taste

Preheat broiler to high.

Carefully clean the kidneys. Cut them in half; remove the fat, the core, and all excess tubes. Rinse in cold water and pat dry on paper towels. Skewer kidneys so they will stay flat during cooking.

Brush kidneys with olive oil and broil for about six minutes on each side. Season with salt and pepper and serve immediately.

Four to six servings

Kelly's Breakfast Casserole

6 slices cubed bread, decrusted
1 pound browned venison bulk sausage
10 ounces grated VERY SHARP cheddar cheese
6 eggs, beaten with one pint half and half
liquid margarine or melted margarine

Place cubed bread in 9 x 13 baking dish. Squeeze liquid margarine over bread. Layer cheese over bread, then sausage. Pour beaten eggs and cream mixture over sausage. Refrigerate over night.

Bake in 350 degree oven for forty minutes or until set and golden brown.

Six servings

Venison Sausage and Egg Casserole

1/2 pound sharp cheese,
   grated
12 teaspoon dry mustard
1/2 teaspoon paprika
1 teaspoon salt
1 cup sour cream
1 pound venison bulk sausage, cooked and drained
10 eggs

Cover bottom of greased 10 x 6 inch baking dish with half of grated cheese.

Mix all seasonings with sour cream and pour half over the cheese. Add crumbled cooked sausage.

Beat eggs and pour over the mixture. Spoon rest of sour cream mixture over eggs and top with remainder of grated cheese.

Bake, uncovered at 325 degrees for twenty to twenty five minutes.

Ten to twelve servings

Sausage Souffle

1 pound venison bulk sausage, cooked and drained
1/2 pound sharp cheddar
   cheese, grated
6 eggs
2 cups milk
12 slices crustless white bread
Optional: green pepper,
   onion, mushrooms

In 9 x 13 greased pan arrange six slices bread. Cover with one half sausage and one half cheese (and optionals). Repeat. Beat eggs and milk. Pour over layers. Refrigerate over night.

Bake at 350 degrees for one hour.

Ten to twelve servings

Sausage and Grits Casserole

1 pound venison bulk sausage
1/2 cup raw grits, cooked (not instant)
1 cup sharp cheddar cheese, grated
1/2 cup chopped ham
3 eggs
3/4 cup milk
1/4 stick margarine
salt and pepper to taste

Brown and drain venison sausage. Place in 8 inch square casserole. Cook grits by directions (stiff-not runny). Add margarine, cheese, and ham to grits. Beat eggs, milk, salt, and pepper together and add to slightly cooled grits mixture. Pour over sausage in casserole. Bake at 350 degrees about forty minutes or until set. Serve immediately.

Four to six servings

Broccoli and Sausage Pie

1/2 pound venison bulk sausage
1 package (10 ounce) chopped broccoli
2 eggs
1 1/2 cups milk
salt and pepper to taste
2 cups grated cheese (try a mixture of Swiss and cheddar)
1 deep dish pie crust, baked

While crust is baking, brown sausage and drain, if necessary. Cook broccoli until tender crisp (three to five minutes); rinse in cold water. Beat eggs and add milk and salt and pepper. Place sausage in cooked crust, then a layer of cheese. Add broccoli and remaining cheese. Pour milk and eggs over top.

Bake at 350 degrees for thirty five to forty minutes or until knife comes out clean in center.

Six servings

Scotch Eggs

1 pound venison bulk sausage
1/2 teaspoon sage (or to taste)
1/2 teaspoon pepper
1/2 teaspoon salt
6 hard-boiled eggs, peeled
1/2 cup canola oil

Lightly mix sausage and seasonings. Remember you can add your favorite seasonings—particularly if sausage is mild. Completely wrap each cooked egg in sausage using several tablespoons of sausage per egg. Place in refrigerator for several hours to allow sausage to set.

Fry eggs in hot oil until browned. Drain well.

This certainly makes a portable breakfast for those early morning hunts.

Six servings

Boiled Eggs and Sausage Casserole

6 hard-boiled eggs, sliced
salt and pepper to taste
1 pound venison bulk sausage
1 jar sliced mushrooms,
  drained
1 1/2 cups sour cream
1/2 cup dry bread crumbs
1 cup grated cheddar cheese
1/2 cup grated Swiss cheese

Slice boiled eggs into buttered casserole and season to taste. Cook sausage and drain, if necessary. Sprinkle sausage over eggs. Layer mushrooms over sausage. (Peppers and onions may be added if desired). Pour sour cream over mushrooms. Combine crumbs and cheese and sprinkle over casserole. Bake in 350 oven until heated through (about thirty minutes). If necessary, brown top under broiler.

Six servings

Corned Venison and Cabbage

**3 pound corned venison roast
  or brisket**
1 onion, sliced
1 garlic clove, minced
1 bay leaf
6 - 8 carrots, cut into chunks
6 - 8 red potatoes, halved
**1 small head green cabbage,
  cut into wedges**

Place corned venison roast or brisket in dutch oven; cover with water. Add onions, garlic and bay leaf. Bring to a boil and simmer for two to two and a half hours or until tender. After tender add carrots and potatoes to pot. Simmer for fifteen to twenty minutes. Add cabbage and cook for fifteen to twenty minutes more or until vegetables are tender.

Slice roast to serve and surround with vegetables. Pour a little cooking liquid over venison.

Serve with hot rye bread.

Eight servings

Venison Liver Paté

1 pound venison liver, cleaned
  and washed
1 onion, chopped
1/3 cup butter (the real thing)
1 ounce sherry
1 teaspoon salt
1/2 teaspoon pepper
2 hard-boiled eggs

Melt butter and sauté liver and onion in butter about ten minutes but be careful and do not over cook. Place in blender or food processor with remaining ingredients and mix until smooth. Taste and adjust seasonings. Refrigerate at least three hours. Serve with assorted crackers or party rye.

Disappearing Paté

1 can chicken broth
1 can water
2 stalks celery, cut into chunks
1 tablespoon parsley
1/2 teaspoon pepper
1 pound venison liver, cleaned
  and washed
1 large onion, sliced
1 teaspoon salt
1 hard-boiled egg
dash of cayenne pepper
1 cup REAL butter, softened
1/2 teaspoon nutmeg
2 teaspoons dry mustard
1/4 teaspoon garlic powder
2 tablespoons brandy

Bring broth, water, celery, parsley, and onion to a boil. Add liver and cook covered about ten minutes. Drain liver and onion well. Remove celery. Chop liver and onion in food processor until smooth. Add remaining ingredients and blend thoroughly. Chill thoroughly and serve with assorted breads or crackers.

Liver with Bacon and Onions

3 - 4 slices bacon
4 - 6 slices (very thin) venison liver
1 onion, sliced
1 cup sour cream
hot cooked rice or pasta

Cook bacon in large skillet until crisp. Reserve drippings. Crumble bacon and set aside.

Sauté liver and onions in drippings. Be careful not to over cook. Remove from pan.

Add sour cream to pan and cook over low heat until heated through. Do not boil. Pour over liver and onions. Sprinkle with bacon. Serve over rice.

Four servings

Liver á la French

1/2 cup flour
1/4 teaspoon garlic salt
1/4 teaspoon salt
1/4 teaspoon pepper
1 pound thinly sliced deer liver
1/2 cup French dressing (commercial)
3 tablespoons canola oil (or bacon drippings)

Combine flour, salts, and pepper. Dip liver slices in French dressing and then dredge in flour mixture.

Cook liver in hot oil (or bacon drippings) until golden brown. Do not over cook and turn only once. Serve immediately.

Four servings

Sour Cream Liver

1 pound venison liver
1/4 cup flour
2 tablespoons melted margarine
3/4 cup chopped onion
1 cup fresh mushrooms,
  sliced
1 garlic clove, minced
2 tablespoons melted margarine
2 - 3 tablespoons flour
1 can (10 ounce) beef consommé
salt and pepper to taste
1 cup sour cream

Dredge liver in flour. Cook in two tablespoons melted margarine until lightly brown. Do not over cook. Remove and set aside to cool. Cut into thin strips.

Add two additional tablespoons margarine to pan and sauté onion, mushrooms, and garlic until tender. Add flour and stir to brown. Stir in consommé and seasonings. Cook until thickened; stir constantly. Add liver and simmer ten minutes. Remove from heat and add sour cream. Return to heat and heat thoroughly but do not boil. Garnish with parsley flakes. Serve over noodles or rice.

Four to six servings

Garlic Liver in White Wine

1 pound venison liver, cut into
  1/2 inch strips
1/3 cup flour (seasoned with
  salt, pepper and paprika)
2 garlic cloves, minced
4 tablespoons margarine
1/2 cup dry white wine
1/2 - 3/4 cup sour cream
1 teaspoon paprika
1 tablespoon dried parsley

Dredge liver in seasoned flour. Melt margarine; add liver and garlic and brown about four minutes. Remove from pan. Add wine and stir to loosen all drippings. Add sour cream, paprika, and parsley. Heat thoroughly but do not boil. Stir in liver and adjust seasonings. Serve over pasta or rice.

Four servings

Sweet and Sour Sausage

1 pound venison bulk sausage
1 pound venison kielbasa, sliced
1 1/4 cups ketchup
1/4 cup dark brown sugar
1 tablespoon soy sauce
1 tablespoon lemon juice
1 can (15 ounce) pineapple chunks, drained

Make small sausage balls and cook in skillet until browned. Drain if necessary. Add kielbasa to sausage balls and simmer. Mix all other ingredients except pineapple and add to sausages. Simmer, covered, about ten minutes. Add pineapple just before serving. Serve in chafing dish.

Sausage Stuffed Mushrooms

20 large fresh mushrooms
1/3 cup margarine, melted
6 ounces venison bulk sausage
3 tablespoons green onions, finely chopped
1 tablespoon fresh parsley, finely chopped
1 clove garlic, minced
salt and pepper to taste
3/4 cup mayonnaise
1/2 tablespoon prepared mustard

Clean mushrooms and remove stems, leaving caps intact. Chop the stems finely and sauté in margarine (about eight minutes). Add onion, parsley, garlic, salt and pepper to taste.

In separate small skillet cook sausage and crumble. Be sure to have it very fine. Add to mushroom mixture and sauté until onion is tender (about five minutes).

Stuff mushrooms with sausage mixture and place in a lightly greased dish. Combine the mayonnaise and mustard and top each stuffed cap with a small blob.

Bake ten to fifteen minutes at 350 degrees.

Serve immediately.

Tip: Try this with minced clams or shrimp stuffing.

Venison Sausage Balls

1 pound venison bulk sausage (raw)

8 ounces sharp cheese (grated)

4 cups Bisquick (be sure to use regular and not lower fat)

Mix sausage and Bisquick thoroughly. Add cheese. Make into balls. Bake on ungreased cookie sheet at 325 degrees for twenty to twenty five minutes or until golden brown. Do not over cook. Will be too hard if cooked too long. These freeze well and can be heated in the microwave as needed.

Tip: The lower fat Bisquick would not stick together enough to make into balls.

Chile Con Queso

1 pound venison bulk sausage
1 onion, chopped finely
1 garlic clove, minced
2 pounds process American
cheese, cut into one-inch
  cubes
1/2 cup milk
1 can (10 ounce) tomatoes and
  green chilies, undrained and
  chopped

Cook sausage, onion, and garlic over medium heat until done. Stir to break apart. Drain well.

Place cheese and milk in top of a double boiler over medium heat until cheese is melted. Stir constantly. Stir in sausage and onions and tomatoes with chilies. Serve warm in chafing dish with tortilla chips.

Mexican Dip

1/2 pound ground venison
1/2 pound venison bulk sausage
1 pound Velveeta cheese,
  chopped
1 jar (16 ounce) salsa

In large skillet brown meats. Add cheese and salsa and stir constantly until cheese melts.

Keep hot (in chafing dish) and serve with tortilla chips.

Tip: 1 can cream of mushroom soup can also be added to dip if you like less cheese flavor or need to stretch the recipe.

Jack's Marinade for Jerky

1 cup soy sauce
1 ounce Worcestershire sauce
1/2 teaspoon pepper
1 teaspoon garlic
1 teaspoon onion powder
1 ounce taco sauce
1/2 ounce Tabasco sauce
1/3 cup brown sugar
1/3 cup salt or cure mix

This is enough marinade for about two and a half pounds venison. Marinate for three days. Place strips of venison on rack in over and cook for ten to twelve hours at 150 - 175 degrees. Store in air tight container.

Jerky

Cut venison into 1/4 inch strips with grain of muscle. Toss with soy sauce and garlic salt until well coated. Place strips on oven rack so that they are not touching. Put in 150 - 175 degree oven for ten to twelve hours. Do not cook until crisp.

Store in air tight container. Little white specks can be cut off and are not harmful.

Suggested Menus:
A Dozen Venison Dinners

One of the most common complaints of those with little acquaintance with venison is that they have no idea of what to serve with the meat. The potential answers to that dilemma are without number, but we thought it might be helpful, in concluding, to provide a few samples of complete menus. A dozen complete meals are offered below, complete with suggested vegetables or fruits, drinks, and dessert. All of the venison recipes come from the cookbook, with two being taken from each section.

Several of them include a suggested wine, and on this score a word or two of advice might be in order. Standard wisdom once held that with venison, and indeed all red meats, only hearty, heavy red wines such as a burgundy were suitable. Thinking has changed considerably in this regard in recent years, and certainly we concur with this altered perspective. If you enjoy a glass or two of wine with a meal, drink what you find palatable as opposed to what some supposed connoisseur deems proper. After all, a heavy red wine can sometimes be overpowering, and you want the wine to compliment your food rather than competing with it.

One

V-8 Juice Cocktail or Bloody
  Mary
Loin Steak with Crab and
  Shrimp Sauce
Fresh Spinach Salad

Hot Crunchy Rolls
Lemon Stickies
White Zinfandel Wine
Coffee

Two

Bourguignon Venison
White and Wild Rice Combo
Steamed Broccoli
Tropical Fruit Salad

Bread Sticks
Chocolate Chess Pie
Burgundy Wine
Coffee

Three

Anna Lou's Crockpot Roast
Roasted Parmesan Potatoes
Garlic Green Beans with
  Slivered Almonds
Sautéed Squash and Vidalia

Onions
Angel Biscuits
Sour Cream Pound Cake with
  Strawberries
Iced Tea or coffee

Four

Crockpot Roast and Vegetab-
  les
Creamy Green Pea Salad
Broiled Fruit with Strawberry
  Honey Glaze

Homemade Onion Cheese
  Bread
Blackberry Cobbler with Ice
  Cream
Summertime Iced Tea

Five

Backstrap in Bacon
Burgers with Tomato Topper
Onion Rolls
Triple Bean Bake

Macaroni Salad
Assorted Pickles and Chips
Homemade Banana Ice Cream
Lemonade

Six

Party Meatballs
Dinner-on-the-Grill
Fresh Broccoli Salad
Layered Fruit Salad

Grilled Ranch French Bread
Triple Chocolate Delight
Iced Cold Beer and Soft Drinks

Seven

Zucchini Soup
Venison Piccata
Garlic Spaghetti
Hunter's Green Salad

Crusty Homemade Bread
Chablis Wine
Butter Pecan Cheesecake
Coffee

Eight

Burgundy Mushrooms
Venison Meat Loaf with
  Spinach and Cheese Stuffing
Oven Baked Potatoes
Chilled Asparagus with
  Mustard Dressing

Luscious Strawberry Salad
Brownie Cake
Iced Tea or Coffee

Nine

Brenda's Souper Stew
Herbed Rice
Zucchini and Tomato Salad

Fresh Fruit Compote
Peanut Butter Cookies
Coffee and Tea

Ten

Venison and Noodle Soup
Apricot Delight Salad
Homemade Corn Bread and
  Butter

Apple Crisp
Spiced Tea

Eleven

Mimosas
Sausage and Grits Casserole
Marinated Cherry Tomatoes
Almond-Curried Fruit

Flaky Biscuits
Strawberry Preserves and
  Peach Butter
Sour Cream Coffee Cake
Hot Tea and Coffee

Twelve

Venison Liver Paté
Assorted Crackers and Party
  Rye
Ribs in Beer
Mixed Vegetable Casserole
Slaw or Cucumber Salad

Grilled Tomatoes
Chilled Mugs of Cold Beer
Caramel Coconut Pie
Tea or Coffee

CPSIA information can be obtained
at www.ICGtesting.com
Printed in the USA
LVHW090824241121
703910LV00006B/6